The Kogan Page Guide to

WORKING IN THE HOSPITALITY INDUSTRY

The Kogan Page Guide to

WORKING IN THE HOSPITALITY INDUSTRY

Catering, travel and tourism, leisure,
and the licensed trade

SECOND EDITION

CAROLINE RITCHIE

KOGAN
PAGE

YOURS TO HAVE AND TO HOLD
BUT NOT TO COPY

First published in 1990
Second edition published in 1999

Kogan Page Limited
120 Pentonville Road
London N1 9JN

© Caroline Ritchie 1990, 1999

British Library Cataloguing in Publication Data

A CIP record for this book is available from the British Library.

ISBN 0 7494 2871 6

Typeset by Kogan Page
Printed and bound by Clays Ltd, St Ives Plc

Contents

Acknowledgements

I would like to thank Russell Joseph – my original co-author – for his help in acting as a sounding board and memory in the production of this book.

Abbreviations used

'A' level	Advanced level (GCE)
ABTA	Association of British Travel Agents
BA	Bachelor of Arts
BII	British Institute of Innkeepers
Bsc	Bachelor of Science
BTEC	Business and Technology Education Council
C	College/Certificate
C&G	City and Guilds
CF&HE	College of Further and Higher Education
CFE	College of Further Education
CHE	College of Higher Education
CNAA	Council for National Academic Awards
CSE	Certificate of Secondary Education
GCE	General Certificate of Education
GCSE	General Certificate of Secondary Education
GMWU	General and Municipal Workers Union
GNVQ	General National Vocational Qualification
HCIMA	Hotel, Catering and International Management Association
HNC	Higher National Certificate
HND	Higher National Diploma
Hons	Honours
HTF	Hotel and Training Foundation
IATA	International Air Travel Association
IHE	Institute of Higher Education
MAp	Modern Apprenticeship
NALGO	National and Local Government Officers Association

Abbreviations used

NC	National Certificate
NCVQ	National Council for Vocational Qualifications
NTC	National Training Certificate
NVQ	National Vocational Qualification
'O' level	Ordinary level (GCE)
OND	Ordinary National Diploma
RIPHH	Royal Institute of Public Health and Hygiene
SCE	Scottish Certificate of Education
SCOTVEC	Scottish Vocational Education Council
SVQ	Scottish Vocational Qualification
TEC	Technical College
U	University
UCAS	Universities and Colleges Admissions Service
WSET	Wine and Spirit Education Trust

Introduction

This book offers factual information about job opportunities in the hospitality and licensed trade industries. The hospitality industry is made up of various sectors – catering, licensed trade, travel, tourism and leisure – as well as important back-up services. No one sector or chapter of this book is self-contained; consequently, all are cross-referenced to enable you to see the similarities of many jobs in varying sectors of the industry as a whole, which is illustrated more comprehensively in the career trees on pages 108–23. For example, a receptionist may work in a hotel, tourism, a travel or leisure centre; a chef may be employed in a hotel, restaurant, industrial or institutional catering, but may also be found in the kitchen of a tourist attraction or on a cruise ship; a human resources manager is required in all large organizations, whatever the sector, to look after the employees, and so on.

As a user of this book, you should start where you think your interests lie and see where this takes you. By using the job descriptions and the career trees you will surely be taken into areas you had not thought of exploring before. Each chapter gives a general description of the work or different jobs in that specific field, the job opportunities, where the jobs are advertised, the career development you might expect, the personal qualities required for this kind of work, salary range, as well as information on union membership and equal opportunities (where relevant), entry requirements, qualifications and training available, professional bodies and sources of further information.

When you find an area of work that interests you, you should try to look at some of the suggested further reading, send for college prospectuses and write to the professional bodies and company recruitment officers. This book is only a starting point. It will not, for example, give you an insight into what it is like to do any of the jobs described; for that you should turn to the books in the Kogan Page 'Careers in' and 'Great Careers' series. These contain case studies, interviews with people in posts who talk about their work and tell you about the realities behind the recruiting literature.

The industry as a whole employs well over 2 million people, making it one of the biggest in the UK. It is also one of the most varied. You can be a bar person in a ski resort such as Chamonix or a five-star hotel such as Gleneagles; or perhaps a receptionist at EuroDisney or on a Caribbean cruise liner; or perhaps a leisure centre manager; or, for the independent minded, eventually you may run your own business, café, restaurant or other establishment.

What do you want to be?

Did you know that many people become managers of a business handling £200,000 or more per year while still in their twenties? Did you know that a housekeeper can earn over £20,000 per year? Did you know that a chef can earn over £25,000 per year? Did you know that a full-time student can win fully paid overseas study tours? Did you know that a bartender can become an area manager within a few years?

Did you know that the hospitality industry is one of the fastest-growing business areas that constantly has job vacancies? Did you know that there is a serious skills shortage within the hospitality industry as it expands at a faster rate than that at which people can be trained up, and that hundreds of new job vacancies will be created next year, and the year after, and the year after?

Do you want to work in the EU, the Bahamas, Australia, America, a ski resort in winter, a 'hot spot' in summer? Do you want to work for the Queen, the Sultan of Brunei, Planet Hollywood, British Airways, Bass, Virgin?

What do you want to do?

Read on to see what you can do now, what qualifications you need to progress, where to get them and how.

Job opportunities

This industry is growing faster than a great many others in the whole of the EU. Thus, you can be certain of getting a job and that it will have good career prospects. The career trees (see pages 108–23) illustrate how people can change sectors within the industry, and the various levels at which they can enter. To get a job you can either remain close to home or travel the world. If you intend to work abroad, it is best to have some internationally recognized qualifications, as mentioned in this book, but, most important of all – in what is essentially a service industry – is your personality. Qualifications (where applicable) will get you to the interview, but your personality will win or lose you the job on the day.

Employee or your own business?

When you are at the beginning of your career, it is a good idea to look for a salaried post as it is reassuring to have a sum of money coming in each month. Many people in the industry work for themselves – some from choice, some from necessity – and the going can be very tough to begin with. If you are making the transition from salaried to self-employed status, plan the move carefully, build up as wide a network of contacts as you can, assemble a business portfolio (or other evidence) of your career to date, consider employing an accountant, find out from the Benefits Agency what your rights and obligations are, take advice on such matters as insurance and pension plans, and prepare a business plan to present to your bank manager or other financial backers. A small business adviser will help you with this.

You have to be completely reliable about business commitments, but it is very easy to take on too much, or the wrong sort, of work because you are afraid to turn down a job and risk losing a potentially useful contact or because you are worried about not making enough money.

Finding work

Jobs within the hospitality and licensed trade industries are advertised widely in specialist publications, such as the *Caterer and Hotelkeeper*, *Travel Trade Gazette*, *Leisure Opportunities* and *The Publican*. The advertisements in these and other such publications will normally be for specialist jobs requiring qualifications. Local newspapers – for example, the London *Evening Standard* – are a good source of information about less skilled jobs and may also carry information on local specialist opportunities. There are also many employment agencies dealing exclusively with the hospitality industry. They normally specialize in one particular area and it is wise to check this out before approaching one. These agencies have a good reputation within the industry.

Letter of application

At the risk of stating the obvious, here are some guidelines.

Make a rough draft of your letter of application and check that it contains all the essential points, and responds directly to any specifications given in the advertisement.

It does not matter if you cannot word process your letter, but it must be neat and legible. However, most people can now gain access to a word processor. If you do not have your own computer, most Job Centres will help you to word process a job application, as will your school, if this is applicable. Your local library may also have word processing facilities that you can use. However you prepare your application letter, you should note the following points.

- Use good-quality, preferably white, writing paper and a matching envelope.
- Never use headed paper that you are not entitled to use.

- Address the letter to the Head of Appointments or Human Resources Manager or Head of Recruiting Department (or some other such person).
- If you know this person's name (you may have seen it in a brochure or leaflet), use it. If you write 'Dear Mr/Ms ...', sign off 'Yours sincerely'; if you do not know their name, write 'Dear sir or madam' and sign off 'Yours faithfully'.
- Type or print your name under your signature.
- Always, when word processing your letter, use both the grammar and spell check facilities. These will enable you to pick up almost all errors. The spell check tool alone may not do this.
- If you have any doubts about spelling or grammar, show your letter to a teacher or a reliable friend or relative (it is probably a good idea to do this in any case).
- Keep a copy of your letter for reference.
- If you are replying to an advertisement, say where you saw it.

Find out all you can about the organization you are applying to. What are its goals, who are its customers?

Be specific about your own interests, skills and experience. It is not enough simply to say that you would like a job in the industry – you must give your reasons for this.

Keep your letter short and make your CV as comprehensive as possible.

Curriculum Vitae

Type your CV (or have it typed) if you possibly can. It is worth paying to have a CV typed professionally (keep the master and make photocopies) – a good typist will know how to set it out and might be able to advise on content and phrasing. Again, your school or local Job Centre will be able to help you create a professional CV. A CV should include your:

- full name and address;
- date of birth;
- schools attended;
- examinations passed (with dates and grades);
- any other honours won at school or college;

- training courses/colleges attended and qualifications gained (again with dates and grades);
- previous jobs held, no matter how briefly, and any other experience (names of employers and dates);
- names and addresses of two referees – one of whom should be a previous employer or someone who has personal knowledge of your abilities;
- personal interests and hobbies, especially those relevant to the job you would like;
- foreign languages – indicate your level of competence (for example, you could say whether you speak/read/write the language);
- driving licence – a clean, current driving licence is needed for many jobs, so if you have one, mention it.

The interview

You may feel very nervous at an interview and find it difficult to collect your thoughts when asked even quite simple and obvious questions. It is a good idea to think about what you would say in answer to questions such as the following.

- Tell me about yourself.
- Why do you want a career in the hospitality/licensed trade?
- What made you apply for this particular job/write to this organization?
- Why do you think you will be good at this job/you have something to offer this organization?
- What attracts you to this job/organization?
- How much do you know about this organization?
- How would you like your career to develop? What would you like to be doing in five/ten years' time?
- (If you already have a job) Why do you want to leave your present job?
- What are your interests outside work, particularly those dealing with people?

Remember that you will be competing for work in an area where personality and commitment count for as much as qualifications.

A degree or recognized diploma will open a few doors, but in the eyes of a potential employer they may well count for less than references from previous employers, even if they were only holiday jobs. Everyone has to start somewhere and, of course, employers do not imagine that work experience is the only proof of ability and interest; they will want to know about your involvement in such things as extra-curricular activities, voluntary work and so on. They will, however, expect you to show some knowledge of the area you are trying to break into. For example, if you are seeking work in a travel agency, you should have a good knowledge of geography. You will have to convince your interviewers that you are fascinated by travel agency work and not give the impression that you are just trying to see if you might like it and fancy some free travel. Similarly, if you apply for a job within the licensed trade, you should be able to show that you are aware of the social problems that can be caused by alcohol as well as being positive about working in that particular environment.

Union membership

There is no tradition of union membership, although in some establishments, particularly where there are many employees, some belong to the General and Municipal Workers Union (GMWU). Many people belong to trade associations or professional bodies; for example, the HCIMA, the British Institute of Innkeeping or the Guild of Sommeliers. In the industrial and public sector, some belong to unions such as the National and Local Government Officers Association (NALGO), which have an interest in these areas. Discrimination against people belonging to unions is rare.

Equal opportunities

Most employers in the UK have an equal opportunities policy, and, given the international nature of the industry, racial discrimination is rare. However, some establishments may have a policy of employing people from one racial group only. For example, in a Japanese restaurant only Japanese people may be employed to give authenticity to the establishment.

The majority of employees within the hospitality industry are women, many of whom work part-time, having arranged the hours to suit themselves. Many women and many members of ethnic minorities are employed in top jobs or own their own companies. All jobs are open to both sexes and all races.

Career development

In some areas, people with talent and ideas can rise rapidly and make a great deal of money. In other areas of the industry, you could spend much longer progressing. Wherever you work, you will have to cope with fierce competition and be able to perform well under pressure. The chances are that you will change jobs/sectors several times. For example, a chef may begin their career in a holiday camp before moving to an hotel, then a restaurant or their own establishment, at home or abroad. An hotel receptionist may work as a guide or resort representative. There are endless possibilities, and experience gained in one field will equip you well to work in another.

Personal qualities

It is essential that you should have an outgoing and extrovert personality. You should like people and enjoy working with them. Do you look presentable at all times? Do you perform well under pressure? Are you a good team member? That is to say, can you be relied on to play your part (however small) competently and produce your work on time? Can you smile in the face of adversity and solve the problem?

Many people have succeeded because, while they have a limited number of academic qualifications, they have agreeable personalities and an ability to work hard under pressure in the public eye, for many, often unsociable, hours.

There are also a great many administrative, back-up and technical posts for which professional competence and technical expertise are needed. These make interesting and satisfying careers for those who prefer not to be in the public gaze quite so much.

Vocational and professional qualifications

In order to practise certain jobs outlined in this book – say management trainee – you have to have certain specific qualifications before you can get a job. In other areas – such as cookery – it is also highly desirable to have professional training, but this is often acquired on a part-time basis and supported by your employer. In other fields – such as bar person – no qualifications are required to start with.

There are certain recognized lead bodies for the hospitality industry. Obtaining their vocational and/or professional qualifications will improve your career prospects. The Business and Technician Education Council (BTEC) and NVQ/SVQ are such bodies. If you are in any doubt about qualifications and training, write to one of the professional bodies or trade associations or to the employer for whom you would like to work. Before you enrol on a course, make sure that it will lead to relevant, recognized/accredited qualifications. There are some private training companies around that run courses not accredited nationally and so they are not recognized by most employers.

There are currently three 'core' sets of qualifications, one of which will be suitable for you. On top of these core courses, you can take various other shorter qualifications that will add value to your overall educational profile. Described below are the three core sets of qualifications and those shorter qualifications that are most valued by employers, or magistrates in the case of the licensed trade.

It should be noted that the core qualifications may be divided into lower and more advanced ones – further education and higher education. The government has accredited each qualification with a level – 1 to 5 – and accreditation at a lower level allows for progression to a higher-level qualification. For instance, an NVQ/SVQ level 3, GNVQ Advanced and two 'A' levels are all accredited at the same level – 3 – and so all can lead to level 4 qualifications – that is, an HND or possibly a degree if the grade awarded for the level 3 qualification is high enough.

The three cores are:

- NVQ/SVQ qualifications;
- BTEC qualifications;
- Degree and postgraduate qualifications.

Each of these is discussed below and the lead bodies that administer each qualification are mentioned.

NVQ/SVQ – National Vocational Qualifications/ Scottish Vocational Qualifications

The government set up the National Council for Vocational Qualifications (NCVQ) in 1986. Its aim was to standardize vocational qualifications (NVQ/SVQ) throughout the UK and enable students to acquire competences at a speed that suited each individual studying for them. NCVQ aims to ensure that its qualifications are based on the requirements of industry and commerce. They are all vocational and primarily work based, but some NVQ/SVQs are taught on a full-time basis at colleges of further education or TECs. NCVQ accredits the wide range of NVQ/SVQs available at four levels:

- Level 1 – operative level, simple tasks;
- Level 2 – operative level, more complex tasks, with some responsibility;
- Level 3 – supervisory level;
- Level 4 – management.

SVQ is the Scottish equivalent of the English and Welsh NVQ. All NVQ/SVQ qualifications consist of mandatory units, units that must be gained for full completion of the qualification, and optional units, where the student can choose which units they would like to take. When the students have accumulated a sufficient number of units, they will be awarded the relevant NVQ or SVQ, such as Food Preparation and Cooking or Guests Service, both of which are level 2 qualifications. Some of the higher-level NVQ/SVQs also include mandatory key skills, and some colleges offer value-added modules that can be taken alongside the NVQ/SVQ to enhance the whole learning process.

From this point on, NVQs and SVQs will be referred to as NVQs unless there is a difference in practice rather than a geographical one.

NVQs are awarded via three main lead bodies and NVQs in specialisms may be awarded by a relevant authorized body.

City and Guilds (C&G)

Normally this awarding body does not have a fixed pre-entry qualification for levels 1 and 2, although some colleges may set some pre-entry tests – usually in the areas of English and maths. For level 3 and above, acquisition of the previous level or equivalent prior learning is usually required. These qualifications can be obtained on a full-time, part-time or day-release basis.

C&G is the lead body used by most colleges of further education. C&G also accredits a series of international awards for overseas students, which run in parallel to NVQ qualifications. For further information, contact City and Guilds at:

1 Giltspur Street
London EC1A 9DD
Tel: 0171 294 2468; fax: 0171 295 2400.

Training and Enterprise Councils (TECs) and Local Enterprise Companies (LECs)

TECs were set up in 1990/1 as a result of a government initiative. Originally there were 81 TECs in England and Wales, each dealing with a given territory, and 22 Local Enterprise Councils in Scotland that fulfil the same role as the TECs. Their purpose is to help local people and local businesses by maximizing their human resource potential in business, enterprise and the local labour market. As a consequence, much of their work is done in partnership with local key agencies – that is, colleges and employers. Due to rationalization, the number of TECs and LECs has been reduced, and the emphasis has shifted to one of training for the needs of the local community, especially for smaller businesses.

By investing in people and businesses, they are able to support the Modern Apprenticeship and National Training Certificate schemes, promote good practice in business, assist businesses with training and development, act as an adviser and provide training. This unique service aids those unemployed and actively seeking employment, people with disabilities and school-leavers or adults looking to retrain.

For further information, contact your local TEC/LEC.

Hotel and Training Foundation (HTF)

The Hotel and Catering Training Company became the Hotel and Training Foundation on 1 May 1996 in order to more accurately reflect and separate the activities previously conducted under one title. The HTF's main role is to improve information about the whole of the hospitality industry and work towards developing qualifications. These activities are supported by three training divisions:

- the Stonebow Group;
- the Hospitality Awarding Body;
- the Hotel and Catering Training Company.

As a commercial venture, they provide support and training materials – mainly to the hotel and catering sectors of the hospitality industry. The Stonebow Group concentrates on offering short courses, training and consultancy services to companies intending to introduce training. The Hospitality Awarding Body awards NVQs and SVQs to trainees. The Hotel and Catering Training Company provides youth and adult training programmes and Modern Apprenticeships.

For further information, apply to the:

Hotel and Training Foundation
International House
High Street
Ealing
London W5 5DB
Tel: 0181 579 2400; fax: 0181 840 6217.

Modern Apprenticeships (MAps)

Modern Apprenticeships are vocationally based and are for those who want to gain qualifications while at work rather than by embarking on a course of full-time study. This means that they are to be found mainly in the hotel, restaurant and licensed trade sectors. The qualifications being worked towards are NVQ based and, although there is no fixed timeframe, most people take between two and three years to acquire the required number of units to gain full accreditation of the appropriate NVQ. All MAps are awarded at level 3 and above and include key skills. Those who are successful are also awarded a Certificate of Modern Apprenticeship from the HTF.

For further information about MAps, contact your local Job Centre, TEC or the HTF.

National Training Certificate (NTC)

This is part of the Welfare to Work Programme, set up by the government. It is very similar to the MAp scheme, but the qualifications being worked towards are at levels 1 and 2.

For further information, you should contact your local Job Centre, TEC or the HTF.

Business and Technology Education Council (BTEC)

BTEC is an assessment and awarding body for NVQ and GNVQ qualifications accredited by NCVQ within the hospitality industry. GNVQs (General National Vocational Qualifications) are more broadly based than NVQs. For instance, at level 3, the GNVQ would be in Hospitality and Catering, while an equivalent NVQ could be Food Preparation and Cooking, Patisserie and Confectionery.

BTEC awards NVQs at levels 1 to 4, in the same way as other lead bodies. However, it is probably better known for its awarding of GNVQs at levels 1 to 3, and for its First Diplomas, National Diplomas, Higher National Certificates (HNCs) and Higher National Diplomas (HNDs). It is the intention of the government to phase out the First and National Diplomas over a period of time and replace them with the appropriate level of GNVQ. This process has already begun. Some subject areas have changed over, some are in transition. The GNVQ Advanced and BTEC National Diploma can lead directly on to higher education.

BTEC and The University of London Examination and Assessment Council have recently combined under the umbrella heading of the 'Edexcel Foundation'. Broadly speaking, BTEC forms the vocational division while Edexcel directly administers the nationally set examinations.

The GNVQ and other qualifications administered by BTEC/EDEXCEL are as follows:

- GNVQ Foundation, level 1 – no entry criteria;
- GNVQ Intermediate – First Diploma – level 2 – no fixed prerequisite entry criteria, but often taken alongside GCSEs;
- GNVQ Advanced – National Diploma – level 3 – equates to two 'A' levels, entry prerequisites are four GCSEs, at grade A, B or C, or four 'O' levels; NVQ level 2 qualifications in an appropriate discipline; GNVQ Intermediate in a related discipline; BTEC First in a related discipline;
- Higher National Certificate (HNC), levels 3 and 4 – as this is normally a part-time mode of study undertaken by mature students, the entry prerequisites are very varied, ranging from no formal educational qualifications but senior employment positions, to perhaps a younger person who, having completed a GNVQ Advanced or National Diploma, chooses to follow a part-time route into higher education rather than a full-time one; each applicant will be looked at on an individual basis and enquiries should be directed towards your local FE or HE college;
- Higher National Diploma (HND), level 4 – the minimum entry prerequisites are as follows: one 'A' level, plus three GCEs at grades A, B or C (or three 'O' levels), normally in subjects that test English and maths/science; GNVQ Advanced or National Diploma in a related discipline; for mature students, entrance via accreditation of prior learning (APL) may be possible.

Applications would be made via the UCAS system (see Degrees). Note that mandatory grants are awarded at HND level.

For further information, contact BTEC at:

BTEC
Central House
Upper Woburn Place
London WC1H 0HH
Tel: 0171 413 8400; Fax: 0171 387 6068.

Alternatively, you can reach EDEXCEL at:

EDEXCEL Foundation
Customer Enquiries Unit
Stewart House
32 Russell Square
London WC1B 5DN
Tel: 0171 393 4444.

BTEC also runs a work experience scheme via the Internet, with over 8000 places, to match students with prospective employers. The address is:

http://www.illumin.co.uk/btec/

Scottish Vocational Education Council (SCOTVEC)

This awarding board is administered in a similar fashion to BTEC, but more emphasis is placed on the individual modular approach. Thus, especially at the lower level, courses may be unique to the individual, although if that individual wants to go on to the higher levels, they may have to conform to an orthodox pattern of modules. Obviously H grades would be substituted for 'A' levels in the entrance criteria.

For further details, contact SCOTVEC at:

SCOTVEC
Hanover House
24 Douglas Street
Glasgow G2 7NQ.
Tel: 0141 248 7900; fax: 0141 242 2244; e-mail:
mail@sqa.org.uk

Degree courses

Degrees are awarded either by the university or by the Council for National Academic Awards (CNAA). There are both national and local entry requirements for courses. However, the basic minimum qualifications are two 'A' levels plus three GCSEs at grades A, B or C in other subjects. Maths or science plus English are usually required, and many places will require a language, especially for international courses. In Scotland, the equivalent requirements are three H grades plus two GCSEs at grades A, B or C. GNVQ Advanced at Merit or Distinction level will replace the requirement for A or H grades.

You apply for a place via the:

Universities and Colleges Admissions Service (UCAS)
PO Box 67
Cheltenham
Gloucestershire GL50 3SF
Tel: general enquiries 01242 222444; applicant enquiries
01242 227788; fax: 01242 221622.

However, you can get a prospectus direct from the establishment you are interested in or from libraries, and from some Job Centres. Note that mandatory awards are made for this level of education.

Postgraduate courses

It should be noted that various universities are now offering postgraduate courses at master and doctorate level. Applications should be made direct to the university.

GCE 'O' levels, 'A' levels, CSE or GCSE

The General Certificate of Secondary Education (GCSE) syllabuses and examinations have now replaced 'O' levels and the CSE in all parts of the UK except Scotland. The new certificates are graded A to G, and grades A to C are equivalent to 'O' level grades A to C and CSE grade 1.

As previously mentioned, other recognized qualifications can also be gained. Some of the most common qualifications and their lead bodies are given below. Some of the qualifications are undertaken on a full-time or distance learning basis, such as the HCIMA ones. Others, however, are often gained as value added units in addition to the main course of study. For example, a person studying for a GNVQ Advanced in Hospitality and Catering qualification may also take the RIPHH Certificate. This type of qualification, except for the HCIMA ones, may also be taken as short courses, and will, in this case, often be run by your local college of further education or TEC. For mature people, the attainment of these relevant and nationally respected short courses can be useful if seeking to gain a qualification via accreditation of prior learning.

It should be noted that the list given below does not cover all possible courses/qualifications. If you want to take a course and are unsure about its status, you should always ask which is the lead body for the course and check what level NVQ/SVQ it equates to. As previously stated, it is also always wise to check with other bodies to ensure that the course is nationally recognized.

Hotel, Catering and International Management Association (HCIMA)

This is the professional association for managers and international managers within the hospitality industry. It is also an internationally accredited examination and awarding body, offering part-time courses and flexible modes of study for those already working in the industry. Its mission is to identify, promote and maintain the highest professional and ethical standards for management education and training in the international hotel and catering industry.

The HCIMA runs two programmes of study for those already at supervisory or management level:

- Professional Certificate – designed for those working at supervisory level in the hospitality industry, with at least two years' previous experience;
- Professional Diploma – designed for managers who normally hold a position involving sectional or departmental responsibilities.

British Institute of Innkeeping (BII)

The BII is, like the HCIMA, both a major professional association for members of the licensed trade and an accredited awarding and examination body. Since 1996, it has launched a series of qualifications – equating to NVQ levels 3 and 4 – aimed at raising and maintaining the national standards within the trade. General short courses offered include:

- Catering Management;
- Financial Management;
- Business Management.

The BII also administers a series of qualifications relating to liquor licensing law and the social aspects of the licensed trade. The holding of the appropriate certificate is becoming a prerequisite by magistrates before a liquor licence will be issued to new applicants. These certificates, from the National Licensee's Certificate Awarding Body, part of the BII, cover On-licences, Off-licences and Part IV Licences.

Various centres have been authorized to run these courses. For further information, contact the BII or the National Licensee's Certificate Awarding Body at:

Park House
24 Park Street
Camberley
Surrey GU15 3PL
Tel: 01276 684449; fax: 01276 23045; e-mail: moffice@bii,org;
Web site: http://www.barzone.co.uk

Wine and Spirit Education Trust (WSET)

WSET is the awarding body for an internationally recognized series of examinations in wines, spirits and liqueurs. The entry requirements are that the student must either be working in the industry or studying for an appropriate qualification with an approved examination body. A prerequisite of the higher courses is the previous attainment of the lower level. All courses have been accredited by NCVQ, and approximate to the following levels:

- WSET Certificate — level 2;
- WSET Higher Certificate — level 3;
- WSET Diploma — level 4.

Those people seeking to obtain these qualifications would be likely to work in the food and beverage area of the hotel sector, in restaurants, such as sommeliers, or in café bars, pubs and so on. Courses are run either by WSET itself or under licence at various colleges. These courses may also be offered as value added units on the appropriate full-time course of study.

For further details, contact WSET at:

Five Kings House
1 Queen Street Place
London EC4R 1XX
Tel: 0171-236 3551; fax: 0171-329 8712

Royal Institute of Public Health and Hygiene (RIPHH)

Within the hospitality and licensed trade industries, health, safety and hygiene are of primary importance. Therefore, many people have RIPHH qualifications.

The Royal Institute, which was formed in 1937, sets, controls and moderates examinations in a wide range of health-related topics, including food hygiene and nutrition. All the qualifications have been accredited by NCVQ:

- Primary Certificate;
- Certificate in Food Hygiene;
- Diploma in Food Hygiene, Advanced Level;
- Certificate in Nutrition and Health.

Most of its courses can be followed on a part-time basis or can be taken as a short course, and the Primary Certificate and Certificate in Food Hygiene are often offered as value-added units on the appropriate full-time course of study.

For further information, contact RIPHH at:

28 Portland Place
London W1N 4DE
Tel: 0171 580 2731; fax: 0171 580 6157.

Chapter 1

Catering

Hotels

Hotels can range in size from 2000 bedrooms to 10 or 12, from 5-star establishments to the very basic; they can be part of an international company, such as Sheraton, with all the opportunities that that implies for travel, or part of a British company, such as Granada, or individually owned. Not all large hotels are part of a group and not all small hotels are privately owned, however. There is more scope for advancement in larger hotels or within company-owned hotels, but if you want to practise or improve a specialist skill, you may find a small, privately owned hotel is right for you. You will also see from the career tables on pages 108–23 how you can change your job to another sector of the industry if you choose.

The jobs

Because the word 'hotels' covers such a wide range of skills it would be difficult to draw up a list of jobs that applies to all hotels, but one thing they do have in common is shift work and unsociable hours. This will often include an early morning start and a late evening finish for five days in the week, including weekends. In a smaller hotel, the manager may also be the owner, personnel manager, accountant and sales manager, whereas in a large hotel or chain these would not only be individual jobs but also merit individual departments. The jobs described below are, therefore, a comprehensive list of all that might be found, but you will have to use your common sense in deciding in what type of hotel the jobs would exist in the form described, and when they would be combined with another job – such as receptionist and telephonist.

Accommodation manager

An accommodation manager is another term used to describe a head housekeeper in a large hotel. The role includes managing a number of staff who clean and maintain the bedrooms and public areas within a hotel. It will also include responsibility for training staff working within the area of the hotel the manager covers and for meeting the departmental budget.

Most accommodation managers will have had previous experience as floor housekeepers and probably C&G, BTEC, NVQ or GNVQ qualifications. Promotion will normally be to assistant manager.

Accountant

See page 91.

Baker

A baker is a specialist chef who may also be a qualified patissier (see page 29). The chef's specialism will be in the production of items such as breads and cakes, but may also be in items such as puddings, petit fours and so on.

In order to work in a hotel, a baker will usually have had previous experience as a commis chef and C&G or NVQ qualifications.

Banqueting manager

A banqueting manager is in charge of the banqueting department of a hotel. The role involves organizing all conferences and functions booked into the hotel. The banqueting manager is responsible for the staff, supply of food and drink, maintenance and finances for this department. An exhibition or conference centre may also employ them.

Previous experience will usually have been as an assistant banqueting manager and/or as a banqueting waiter. A banqueting manager will normally have C&G, BTEC, NVQ or GNVQ qualifications.

Banqueting porter

A banqueting porter is employed within a banqueting department to move equipment and furniture when necessary. Much of the work is carried out during unsociable hours. The porter usually has no qualifications but may be working towards an NVQ in order to progress.

Banqueting waiter

Most banqueting waiters are employed on a casual basis, but some – the most senior or those who are on training schemes for supervisory or managerial roles – will be employed full-time. They will work irregular hours whenever there is a function at which their services are required.

Casual banqueting waiters often have no qualifications and no promotional prospects. Full-time staff, however, usually have C&G or NVQ qualifications and may well be working towards a BTEC/GNVQ qualification.

Bar manager

See page 83.

Bartender

See page 83.

Butcher

A butcher, within the hotel environment as opposed to the high street, is a specialist chef who does much of the work of a larder chef.

A butcher will always have specialist C&G or NVQ qualifications as well as a lot of experience.

Cashier

A cashier is responsible for receiving cash from guests. The role may also include responsibility for banking cash.

A cashier may be a member of the reception, front-office or restaurant team. In each case, the cashier will have either C&G, NVQ or GNVQ qualifications and, in order to progress to management levels, BTEC qualifications and experience will be needed.

A cashier may also be employed in the accounts department of many types of establishment. See also page 93.

Cellar person

See page 84.

Chef

A chef is a person who prepares and cooks food for the general public. There are many thousands of establishments that employ chefs of varying levels of skill.

Chefs just starting out in their profession and those who do not intend to be promoted from an establishment providing very basic food, such as a burger van, will have no qualifications; all other chefs will have C&G or NVQ qualifications of varying degrees of specialization. Those wishing to progress will normally take NVQ qualifications either part-time or via MAp or NTC. Most chefs will also have RIPHH or other hygiene qualifications.

Client services manager

See Guest services, page 26.

Cocktail person

See page 84.

Concierge

This is another name for a hall porter. See page 26.

Conference organizer

This is the person who is responsible for the daily administration of conferences and other events run within the establishment. A conference organizer must have good administrative skills, be a good salesperson and able to communicate and manage other people. They must also enjoy working irregular and unsociable hours.

A conference organizer usually has BTEC or degree qualifications and progression is either to hotel management or to a specialist conference company.

Cook

Traditionally women were called cooks and men were called chefs. This is no longer true. Therefore, see Chef, above.

Executive chef

An executive chef is in charge of the kitchen/s and, in a large enough establishment, may not actually cook any more, though most prefer to. This is a managerial position gained only after many years of working in the trade. An executive chef will be

responsible for the staff in their area, the quality of work, maintenance of hygiene, and the departmental budget. They are also
likely to have direct responsibility for the stores area.

An executive chef will have had much experience in most of the
specialist chef areas (see career tree on page 115) and be highly
qualified, with C&G or NVQ qualifications and probably hygiene
and first aid qualifications as well.

Food and beverage manager

This managerial position entails responsibility for the entire food
and beverage operation within an hotel or other establishment,
such as a cruise ship or theme park. A food and beverage manager
will be in charge of food production areas, food service areas and
beverage service areas (both alcoholic and non-alcoholic). They
will be responsible for all the staff, work standards, the budget
and maintenance.

A food and beverage manager will usually have BTEC, degree
or HCIMA qualifications and have worked in either restaurants
or bars; they may also have started their career as a management
trainee. They may also have BII, WSET and/or RIPHH
qualifications.

Front-office manager

This is a senior managerial position that usually leads to general
management.

A front-office manager will have had a great deal of experience
as a receptionist, cashier, reservations clerk and telephonist and
will also be able to train and hire new staff. Such a manager will
also have sales and personnel skills that will enable them to run
the whole of the reception area, and keep within the departmental budget. They will normally have BTEC, degree or HCIMA
qualifications gained on a full- or part-time basis.

Guest-house manager

A guest-house manager's job is best described as all the other jobs
in this section rolled into one. This is because most guest-houses
are privately owned and either were or still are private houses.
Thus, the manager is usually the owner, cook, bar person and so
on, with help from one or two paid employees and the family.

Most guest-house managers have craft (C&G or NVQ) qualifications and most of those new to the business usually take managerial qualifications (BTEC) as well.

Guest services

People involved in guest services are employed primarily in the larger or more prestigious establishments. Their purpose is to solve guests' problems on a personal, one-to-one basis, such as liaison with the kitchen over special dietary needs or arranging translators for business meetings.

Normally, a guest services employee will have started their career in the reception department and will progress into either sales or personnel management. They may also be a management trainee. They will have NVQ qualifications and may also have, or be taking, BTEC ones in order to progress.

Hall porter

This is a much more responsible position than is generally acknowledged. A hall porter is responsible for carrying the guests' bags, as well as for the security of the room keys, arranging transport for the guests and, if there is no ticket agency on the premises, they also book theatre and concert tickets. A hall porter may also look after left luggage and lost property and run certain errands for the guests.

A head hall porter will be in charge of all the porters and be responsible for their honesty and reliability. Although most hall porters are unqualified, a head porter usually belongs to the Société des Clefs d'Or (the Society of Golden Keys). More junior hall porters would now usually take a relevant NVQ to progress.

Hotel manager

This is a senior management position, only gained after years of experience within the industry and initial BTEC, degree or HCIMA qualifications.

A hotel manager will generally have one or two specialist areas of knowledge reflecting past experience, such as food and beverages or front of house. A manager is responsible for the smooth running and financial success of the business and has the overall control of the hotel in their charge.

Housekeeper

A housekeeper is in charge of all the accommodation and public areas of the hotel. This covers such things as cleaning the rooms, their maintenance, overseeing the laundry (uniforms throughout the hotel as well as linen for the restaurants and bedrooms) and hiring, training and firing the departmental staff. A housekeeper must be able to work within the financial constraints of a budget as well as having expert knowledge of the science of cleaning and hygiene.

A housekeeper will normally have progressed from room maid to assistant housekeeper to housekeeper, and have C&G/NVQ qualifications or will have joined the department at assistant housekeeper level and have BTEC, degree or HCIMA qualifications. These qualifications will be necessary if the housekeeper wants to progress on to the general management ladder.

Human resources manager

See page 95.

Kitchen porter

A kitchen porter washes the pots and dishes for the hotel or restaurant kitchen. They are also, along with the chefs, responsible for the day-to-day cleanliness and hygiene of the kitchen.

Although most kitchen porters are unqualified, knowledge of hygiene is useful as is the ability to work in a hot, damp atmosphere. This job is often regarded as one of very low status, yet it is also one of the most important. The normal career progression would be for a kitchen porter to gain an NVQ qualification, as well as qualifications in hygiene, and then progress to a junior chefing position.

Larder chef

A larder chef is head of a section – a senior position within the kitchen brigade. Besides having the skills of a butcher (see page 23), a larder chef must also be skilled in the preparation of fish, the production of salads and other cold items, such as sandwiches.

A larder chef must also have a good knowledge of all basic cookery skills and, thus, have experience and a number of higher-level C&G/NVQ qualifications. Such a chef would also have RIPHH or other hygiene and food safety qualifications.

Licensee

This is the person in the hotel who holds the liquor licence for the premises. It is likely to be the hotel manager or food and beverage manager. The licensee will hold BII or equivalent qualifications. For further details about other kinds of licensee, see Chapter 4, The licensed trade (page 79).

Linen-keeper

A linen-keeper works within the housekeeping department, having responsibility for the linen and uniforms, issuing clean and receiving back dirty laundry. The role may also include doing some of the repairs as well as the stocktaking.

A linen-keeper will usually be unqualified, but may be taking NVQ qualifications in order to progress to assistant housekeeper.

Linkman

A linkman is similar to a trainee hall porter, doing the more basic jobs, such as opening car doors, parking cars, hailing taxis, sheltering guests from the rain with umbrellas and holding open the hotel doors. They usually have no initial qualifications, but can progress to hall porter or receptionist after obtaining a relevant NVQ or NTC.

Management trainee

A management trainee can be found in any area of an hotel at junior management or supervisory level. After leaving college, most students are taken on by a company on a management training programme, which will last between 6 and 12 months, during which time the trainees will gain practical management experience in several different departments. At the end of the training period, a management trainee will be given a junior management position.

A management trainee will always have BTEC, HCIMA or degree qualifications, and may also have some value-added qualifications, such as NVQs, GNVQs, WSET, BII or RIPHH.

Night manager

The position of night manager is often used as a stepping stone to hotel manager. The job is essentially the same except for two areas. First, as the hotel is usually much quieter at night there are fewer demands on the manager. Second, because it is much quieter, a larger proportion of the management accounts are done during this shift. See also Hotel manager, page 26.

Because this is a junior management position, it is often a first permanent job for an employee who has completed their management training. Therefore, although some people will have worked their way up, many will enter with HND or degree qualifications. See also Management trainee, page 28.

Night porter

As with the night manager, the night porter's job is a stepping stone to head hall porter. Except in large hotels, the night porter will be the only porter on duty, so all the jobs that might be shared out during the day will have to be done by them. They may well have other tasks as well, such as buying and sorting the morning papers and making several security checks around the whole building to guard against fire and theft. See also Hall porter, page 26.

Night receptionist

A night receptionist is a senior receptionist who is intending to progress to a junior management position within the front of house area, and sees the responsibility of running the reception area alone as a step in this direction. See also Receptionist, page 30.

Patissier

This is a specialist chef who will have extensive C&G/NVQ qualifications in bakery and pastry work. Such a chef will probably have done some work as a commis chef in other areas of the kitchen. The patissier will be in charge of the production of bakery, pastry work and confectionery for the hotel. This is a particularly prestigious craft on the Continent, and if you intend to pursue a career as a patissier you may find learning another language, particularly French, useful.

Porter

A porter is the shorthand version of either hall porter or kitchen porter. See Hall porter, page 26, or Kitchen porter, page 27. Occasionally the term may be used to refer to a banqueting porter (see page 22).

Public relations Manager
See page 96.

Receptionist
A hotel receptionist will do a variety of jobs depending on the size, location and type of hotel, as well as the market it attracts. For example, a receptionist in a small country hotel will perform a number of tasks that are different from those performed by a receptionist in a large city centre hotel. The one will answer telephones, take reservations, make pots of tea for guests, check guests in and out and so on, while the other may have only one task, such as handling guest arrival. Most will work shifts, usually from 7 am to 3 pm or from 3 pm to 11.00 pm. Dealing with guests on a personal level is an important aspect of the job and means that appearance and social skills are extremely important. A receptionist must also be aware of the capabilities of all the departments within the hotel and act as a salesperson, promoting the hotel's facilities.

All receptionists will have NVQ qualifications in order to progress to shift leader or head receptionist. They may well take BTEC or HCIMA qualifications to further their career to a managerial level.

Recruitment officer
See page 97.

Reservations clerk
A reservations clerk will be found in a large hotel that has a separate reservations department. This department usually operates during the normal working week, with regular office hours. The reservationist offers and accepts bookings and completes necessary records and charts to maintain maximum occupancy levels, as the hotel relies on full occupancy to maximize its profit.

Like a receptionist, a reservations clerk has to be a salesperson and so will often encourage guests to have more exclusive accommodation.

Reservations and reception experience are both required in order to progress to shift leader or head receptionist. Qualifications are similar to those of a receptionist. See also Receptionist, above.

Restaurant manager
Although there is always a restaurant, with a manager, in every hotel, the job can also be considered in its own right. See also page 36.

Room attendant
A room attendant cleans the bedrooms and bathrooms of a hotel. They may also make the room service breakfasts and clean public areas. The hours are from about 7 am to 3 pm, except in 5-star or airport hotels where service may be needed around the clock.

Most room attendants are unqualified, but may take NVQ or BTEC qualifications to progress.

Sales and marketing manager
See page 98.

Silver service waiter
See page 36.

Sommelier
See page 37.

Sous chef
This job is a transition between a specialist chef (a chef de partie), in charge of a single area of the kitchen, and the head chef. In the absence of the head chef, the sous chef will undertake to run the kitchen, and when the head chef is on duty they will deputize for an absent chef de partie.

To hold this position, the sous chef will have had many years of experience within the industry and C&G/NVQ and hygiene qualifications.

Storekeeper
This is the person who looks after the stores for the entire hotel. It is a responsible position, which involves receiving deliveries, making sure that they are what was ordered, in satisfactory condition and, in the case of frozen goods, at the right temperature (to prevent food poisoning). Having been received, the goods – from toilet paper and soap to champagne and caviar – must then be stored correctly to prevent deterioration, theft and contamination. The storekeeper must issue the goods internally on request

and keep financial records of their movement for the accounts department.

Storekeepers are usually unqualified and if they want to progress they normally do so to a clerical position within the accounts department. A storekeeper wishing to progress would usually take relevant NVQ or BTEC qualifications. See also Catering clerk, page 41.

Switchboard operator
See Telephonist, page 99.

Valet
See page 51.

Vegetable chef
This is one of the more junior chef positions. Thus, a newly qualified (NVQ) chef is considered skilled enough to have their own section, but not one of the more senior ones, such as larder. This section used to be regarded as the least important, but with the increasing number of vegetarians and greater interest in healthy eating, this is no longer true.

A vegetable chef will have basic NVQ qualifications and will probably take higher-level, specialist ones in order to progress to chef de partie.

Vegetarian chef
This is a chef who specializes in vegetarian cookery. Such a chef will not normally work in an hotel unless it caters for a large vegetarian community – for example, a Jewish, Muslim or Hindu one. A vegetarian chef is more usually found in a hospital or specialist restaurant.

This chef will have relevant NVQ and hygiene/food safety qualifications.

Waiter
See page 37.

Wine waiter
Another term for a highly skilled wine waiter is sommelier. See pages 37 and 38.

Restaurants

The restaurant industry closely resembles the hotel industry; in fact, many restaurants are part of an hotel. Other restaurants may be privately owned and specialize in a particular style of cooking, while others could be one of several outlets within the same theme park. The range of restaurants is huge, varying from a pizzeria, which may be part of a chain and have up to 200 seats, to a small, privately owned cafe with seats for 20, to a high-class restaurant with French cuisine. The customers vary as well: business people who pay the bill on the company account and not out of their own pockets, pensioners who have to think about the cost of a toasted sandwich, families with children who need space and special children's menus, parties who want to celebrate noisily and so on. The cost of a meal can range from £5 to £100 plus per person, and with it the quality of the restaurant. It is a varied industry; some people opt to work for companies that have a structured career scheme, others decide to work within one style (classical French cuisine, perhaps), others still to work in hotel restaurants and eventually progress to hotel management (or from pub restaurant to pub management), and yet others decide to set up on their own. Some people will work in all these areas.

The jobs

As the hotel and restaurant industries are so closely linked, many jobs exist in both sections. In the restaurant section, all the jobs are listed, but only those with different skills or skills peculiar to the restaurant industry are described in detail. To prevent duplication, the others are cross-referenced to help you to look them up. As in the hotel section, you will have to decide in what kind of establishment the jobs are to be found in their pure form and when they will be combined with another.

Accounts manager
Although bookkeeping is necessary within a restaurant, unless the restaurant is part of a chain and/or an hotel, the establishment will not normally be large enough to justify paying a full-time accountant. The manager/owner will normally do the day-to-day accounting and have the annual accounts prepared by

a firm of accountants. For further details of the work of a catering accounts manager, employed on a full-time basis, see page 91.

Bar manager
See page 83.

Bartender
See page 83.

Cashier
A specialist cashier is only employed in the larger, more up-market restaurants. Besides having a purely cashiering function (see page 23), the cashier will also act as a telephonist (see page 99) and receptionist (see page 30).

Cellar person
This position only exists in a large complex with many bars. See page 84.

Chef
See page 24.

Cocktail person
See page 84.

Cook
See page 24.

Executive chef
See page 24.

Fast food manager
A fast food establishment is one where there is a limited menu, most of the food is already prepared and/or cooked in advance, the average price per person is under £10, it is either self-service or plate service or a combination of the two, the length of the meal is less than half an hour and the customer turnover is high. It often also has a take-away service. Restaurants falling into this category include McDonalds and Pizza Hut.

The job of a fast food manager is similar to that of a restaurant manager (see page 36), except that a fast food manager is likely to have knowledge of only one type of fast food operation and will often have been promoted internally. The next step will be to regional management.

Most people in this position have BTEC qualifications, but may also have NVQ and or RIPHH qualifications.

Fast food operative
Fast food operatives work in the kitchens, behind the service counter or in the restaurant. Normally, they have no entry skills and are trained to do one specific job, such as make pizza bases, fry chips or clear tables. Once they have mastered that skill an operative is trained to learn another, enabling them to gain a relevant NVQ along the way. The operative may be following a MAp or NTC scheme.

To become a fast food manager, an operative has to become familiar with every job in the establishment and acquire management skills, including gaining BTEC qualifications.

Food and beverage manager
This position is unlikely to occur in a single restaurant. It is normally found in establishments with several food service areas, such as hotels' conference/exhibition centres or theme parks.

Usually a restaurant manager will have been promoted to look after several outlets. This is a middle management position. See page 25.

Human resources manager
See page 95.

Kitchen porter
See page 27.

Licensee
See page 28.

Management trainee
See page 28.

Patissier
See page 29.

Receptionist

A receptionist's job in a restaurant varies from that of a hotel receptionist (see page 30) in that the bookings taken are for tables, not rooms. It is similar in that guests' foibles and preferences must be remembered and a high degree of sales and social skills is required.

Most receptionists have C&G/NVQ qualifications. See also Cashier, page 23.

Restaurant manager

This is a middle management position that can lead to hotel, unit or regional management. The restaurant manager has responsibility for the entire restaurant. They are not normally directly responsible for the kitchen, but work closely with the head or executive chef on matters such as menu content, pricing and departmental budgets. A restaurant manager also supervises the maintenance, staffing and quality of service within their area. They need to have good social skills to deal with the restaurant's varied customers, plus a knowledge of sales and marketing in order to promote the establishment.

A restaurant manager will normally have risen from the rank of waiter, have extensive knowledge of alcoholic beverages and have gained much experience in similar-style restaurants in Britain and abroad. A second language is very useful. All restaurant managers will have NVQ qualifications; many others – especially those aiming for senior management – will have BTEC or HCIMA qualifications as well as relevant BII, WSET and or RIPHH qualifications.

Silver service waiter

This is a highly skilled waiting position. A silver service waiter will perform all the duties of an ordinary waiter (see page 37), but have extra skills. These skills include the ability to transfer food from silver dishes to the customer's plate, at the table, in such a fashion as to ensure that the customer feels special and looked after, and is served appetizing food at the correct temperature. The waiter may also be trained in gueridon work. This is the ability to prepare dishes in the restaurant in front of the customers, including crêpe suzette, lobster Newburg and melon au porto. A silver service waiter will also have a good knowledge of alcoholic beverages.

The promotion route is to restaurant manager after the waiter has gained several years of experience in Britain and abroad. All silver service waiters have NVQ qualifications and many have also taken some WSET qualifications.

Sommelier
This is another term for a wine waiter. However, a sommelier normally has much higher-level skills than a wine waiter does. Besides having general knowledge about the service of wines and other alcoholic beverages, sommeliers will have made a special study of the history, manufacture, storage, care and taste of wines. They will be able to describe in great detail any wine in the establishment and many others. They will also help customers to choose the wine/s that will best complement the food they have chosen. The sommelier will usually be closely involved in the purchasing and storage of wines and in updating the wine list. Sommeliers are generally employed only in top-class restaurants where the sale and price of the wine justifies their skill; a rare bottle may sell for over £1500.

A sommelier is likely to have C&G/NVQ qualifications, will definitely have taken some of the WSET qualification and may be a member of the Guild of Sommeliers.

Storekeeper
See page 31.

Vegetable chef
See page 32.

Vegetarian chef
There is an increasing number of vegetarian restaurants and so the number of chefs specializing in this area is growing, as are their skills. Many vegetarian chefs own, or are partners in, the restaurant in which they work. See also page 32.

Waiter
A waiter serves food to customers. They may be highly skilled, as in the case of a silver service waiter (see page 36), or semi-skilled, and just place plates of food in front of the guests. An ordinary waiter still needs many skills, such as an exceptional memory to remember what each customer orders and, if they are regulars,

their likes and dislikes. A waiter must be able to smile and be pleasant under pressure, be discreet and have good sales skills to encourage customers to be adventurous or promote special items. Many people take jobs as waiters on a part-time basis to boost their income and so will be employed as banqueting waiters (see page 23) and in restaurants with lower standards of customer care.

Restaurants generally expect their permanent staff either to have, or be taking, NVQ qualifications. If a waiter intends to progress to management level, they may also take BTEC or HCIMA qualifications on a full- or part-time basis.

Wine waiter

This is the person in a restaurant who serves drinks at the meal table. A wine waiter will serve alcoholic and soft drinks, will have a reasonable knowledge about the service and care of all beverages and should have some knowledge of the wines in the establishment and be able to recommend wines to complement your meal. A wine waiter may have originally been a waiter who has decided to specialize in this area to extend their skills, particularly if they want to progress to head waiter or sommelier (see page 37). Like any other member of staff who comes into contact with the public, a wine waiter must have highly developed sales and social skills.

Most wine waiters have NVQ qualifications and may well be in the process of gaining others, particularly the WSET and BII ones.

Industrial and outside catering

These two areas are looked at together because they have many operational similarities, and the same company may operate in both areas. For instance, Letherby and Christopher holds the concession for the food and beverage operations at White Hart Lane football ground, but it also caters for many outside functions, such as the Cheltenham Gold Cup races held annually in March at the Cheltenham Racecourse in Gloucestershire.

'Industrial catering' is generally taken to mean catering within businesses, such as industrial canteens or directors' dining rooms, where the contract to provide the food may last for several years. 'Outside catering' is generally taken to mean function and exhibition work where a caterer, with all their equipment, food and staff, has to travel to a venue, produce and serve there and then take everything home again at the end of the event. The event may last for one day – such as a grand wedding in a large marquee somewhere – or several days – for example, providing the catering for Wimbledon.

Industrial catering can range from simple works canteens, to self-service restaurants for all levels of staff, to directors' dining rooms with full silver service, to banqueting rooms where guests and VIPs can be entertained to cocktails and canapés or formal dinners. Therefore, the skills of the staff required will vary tremendously from one establishment to another. Sometimes the business does not employ the catering staff directly, but uses an outside catering company, such as Sutcliffe or Gardner Merchant. Others have their own in-house catering facilities, such as The Post Office and Quadrant Catering.

The hours of work for some industrial caterers are normal office hours – 9–5, 5 days a week, with occasional overtime at night – but others may work where the catering operation goes on 24 hours a day, 7 days a week – for instance, in hospitals, power stations or oil rigs. Here there may be chefs employed during the day to prepare food that is held in chilled conditions for the staff at night/weekends that they heat up themselves in a microwave oven during their breaks. This ensures that they have freshly cooked meals at any time of the day or night. However, other establishments may find it more efficient to keep their food production and service areas open at all times.

While providing an industrial catering service, many companies also provide outside catering services. This could mean taking over the catering facilities at the Birmingham Exhibition Centre for the duration of the Clothes Show Exhibition or providing all the meals, with all the special dietary requirements, for the Olympics or providing the catering for the Earls Court Boat Show or erecting a tent in a field at Henley providing one meal only or three meals a day for a week. In this area of the industry, there is a lot of change each day and for each event.

The jobs

Many of the jobs are similar to those described in the hotel and restaurant sections. Those special to this sector are described in detail, the others being cross-referenced to prevent duplication. In this sector, career prospects are different. This is because one company may have many units, but each one may be in a different building. Once someone has progressed to unit management level – which is on a par with someone who is both a head chef and a restaurant manager – the next career step is to area management. In an hotel, this step is normally to senior management, which is on the same level as regional management, the next step up in industrial/outdoor catering management.

Accounts manager
See page 91.

Banqueting manager
See page 22.

Banqueting porter
See page 22.

Banqueting waiter
Apart from hotels and banqueting suites, this is the section of the catering industry where most of the casual waiting staff are employed. See also page 23.

Bar person
In this section of the industry, the job of bar person may be much more responsible than normal. This is because the bar person will also have to look after their stock while it is in transit, store it securely in what might turn out to be a tent and set up the right conditions in which to serve it. See also page 83.

Bartender
See Bar person above and page 83.

Cashier
See page 93.

Catering clerk

Much of the paperwork in an industrial catering unit is completed by a catering clerk. Many college leavers hoping to move into a managerial position often find this a stepping stone between craft and managerial jobs. As a supervisor, a clerk will complete orders and invoices, prepare cash floats and generally be accountable for cash handling.

An NVQ qualification in a craft-based subject in addition to industrial catering experience or a BTEC qualification in Hospitality Management is often an entry to this area. Promotion is often to unit management.

Catering manager

This is another job title given to a unit manager (see also page 44). It may also be used to describe a unit manager who looks after several units but does not have enough seniority to be classed as an area manager.

Conference organizer

It is quite normal for a conference organizer to arrange functions away from their main office. In many ways, their job then becomes similar, administratively, to that of a contract caterer (see below). The organizer will need to have a lot of information about potential venues and their facilities and be prepared to do a great deal of travelling. This is both to meet clients and also to visit the venues at which the clients' events will be held. See also page 56.

Conference secretary

A conference secretary does not always hold specialist qualifications within the catering sector, but may well have receptionist qualifications (see page 30).

A conference secretary supports a conference organizer (see above) by running the office and acting as a point of contact for the conference organizer, clients and venues. If they want to progress, they would normally take relevant BTEC qualifications.

Contract caterer

The manager or owner of a small business is often called a contract caterer if they work in this sector of the industry or if they specialise in providing food and beverages. If they provide facilities for events such as exhibitions, fashion shows and so on plus refreshments, they are likely to be called social events organizer or conference organizer (see pages 41 and 71). They are the person who the client comes into contact with, the person with whom the client arranges the final details, the person responsible for checking the venue to see what types of function and menu would be feasible in that location, and ensuring that all the food and drink, production and service equipment, and staff arrive and are collected from the venue. They may well oversee the function or it might be supervised by an assistant or trainee manager.

A contract caterer will normally have NVQ, GNVQ or BTEC qualifications, plus lots of experience. A good contract caterer needs to be able to work on their own initiative; if, for example, they are finishing work in a mansion in Lincolnshire at midnight and the transport does not arrive, they will have to arrange for everyone to get home because there is no one else to do it. They must therefore be able to remain calm in a crisis or when under stress and have good social skills to be able to deal closely with the clients. They will either own the company or expect their career to progress to area management level.

Cook
See page 24.

Dining room manager
A dining room manager is similar to a restaurant manager (see page 36). Both are responsible for the running of a food service area. However, a dining room manager is usually responsible for one or more rooms that are used by the senior management of the company and booked in advance for a specified number of people eating from a set or limited menu. The customers do not normally pay for their meal at the time, it being one of the perks of their job or a business lunch. The menus are often arranged during discussion with the management concerned.

A dining room manager also looks after the wines and other beverages. Office hours – 9—5 – are the normal working hours.

In small companies, a dining room manager may also be the chef, in which case they will spend a great part of the day working on their own. If the catering is being done by a contract catering company, there may be clear progression ladders to unit or area management. Otherwise, dining room managers may well set up their own contract catering company.

Executive chef
See page 24.

Fast food manager
See page 34.

Food and beverage manager
See page 35.

Industrial caterer
There is no such job as an 'industrial caterer'. It is a term used to describe anyone who works in the industrial sector in a managerial or supervisory capacity. Therefore, both the catering manager for the Bank of England and the area manager for Compass Services could describe themselves as industrial caterers because they have decided to make their careers within this specific sector of the catering industry.

Kitchen porter
See page 27.

Licensee
See page 85.

Management trainee
See page 28.

Outside caterer
This term is used to describe a contract caterer if they only take on functions on a one-off basis. Thus, the person who holds the contract to provide lunches every day for a business' employees is a contract caterer, while the person who wins the contract to organize the twenty-first birthday party for Prince William will be an outside caterer. See also page 41.

Personnel manager
See page 96.

Recruitment officer
See page 97.

Sales and marketing manager
See page 98.

Silver service waiter
See page 36.

Storekeeper
See page 31.

Unit manager
This is a person who is in charge of a whole unit, running both the food production and food service areas. This type of job is generally found in a place such as a self-service industrial restaurant, where there is a full complement of kitchen staff, but only counter assistants and other domestic staff in the food service area.

A unit manager will normally have progressed from the kitchen area or have come in as a management trainee. They will usually have C&G, NVQ and/or BTEC qualifications.

Vegetable chef
See page 32.

Vegetarian chef
See page 32.

Waiter
See page 37.

Wine waiter
See page 38.

Public-sector catering

Public-sector catering is also known as institutional catering. The term is used to refer to organizations where catering is not the main concern of the establishment but is still an essential part of it, such as hospitals. If a patient in hospital does not receive the right food, their recovery will be hindered, and if a child in a children's home does not receive a properly balanced diet, they could become undernourished, with all the accompanying illnesses, such as rickets, that that implies.

Major employers in this sector are hospitals, children's homes, old people's homes, meals on wheels, prisons, schools and colleges of further and higher education.

In this sector, nutrition plays an important role because most people only have access to the food provided by the institution, so it must provide most, if not all, of the dietary requirements for each of them. The diet required by a child, with plenty of protein to help them grow, is not the same as that of a 90-year-old with a weak digestive system or of a healthy adult confined within the prison system.

The workforce may vary greatly from one institution to another. In prisons, most of the work will be done by the inmates, who are usually unskilled, under the supervision of professional chefs and catering managers. In children's homes, the older children will be encouraged to help with the provision of meals, while small children will need to have their meals cooked for them. In hospitals, the patients cannot come to a restaurant, so the food has to be brought to them; in an old people's home, there is normally a plate service system; and in a school, self-service is the norm.

Qualifications

Those entering the public sector at craft level may have no qualifications or NVQ-based ones. Those entering at supervisory level will have GNVQ, HND or degree-level qualifications. Most employees, at whatever level, will have RIPHH or other hygiene and food safety qualifications, such as those of the Institute of Environmental Health Officers (IEHO) or the Royal Society of Health.

The jobs

Many jobs are interchangeable with other sectors, such as restaurants. However, there are some jobs that relate specifically to this sector and they have been described in detail; other jobs are cross-referenced to prevent duplication. There is no normal working pattern within this sector; some people may work 5 days a week, 9–5, others may do shift work to include weekends and nights. Most people, however, work between the hours of 6 am and 9 pm for 5 days a week (which will sometimes include weekends) on a shift and rota basis.

Accounts manager
See page 33.

Chef
See page 24.

Cook
See page 24.

Diet chef
A diet chef specializes in ensuring that the food their customers eat has the correct dietary content for them. They will devise dishes and menus that will provide all the vitamins, minerals, proteins and so on necessary to enable children, patients, adolescents etc to eat a healthy, balanced diet. In a large institution, a diet chef may work alongside a nutritionist (see page 48) and their main task may be simply to devise new menus. In a small institution, they may well do a lot of the cooking and hold a position similar to that of a head chef (see page 24).

Either way, a diet chef will have NVQ, BTEC or degree qualifications and probably have experience as a chef in a restaurant or hotel kitchen.

Domestic services manager
This position is found in large, residential establishments, such as hospitals and universities. It is similar to the position of accommodation manager (see page 22), but with even more emphasis on hygiene, especially in hospitals. A domestic manager will be working under tight budgetary controls with little scope for error.

They will always have qualifications such as BTEC or a degree and may have started as an assistant domestic services manager or management trainee.

Executive chef
See page 24.

Hospital caterer
This position is a combination of unit manager (see page 44) and nutritionist (see page 48). Not only must the staff be fed, which is similar to any unit catering position, but also the patients, most of whom are bedridden and all of whom are ill. A hospital caterer has to ensure that all the ethnic and dietary needs of up to 2000 sick people are met, 3 times a day, and that the food reaches the wards, which may be 20 minutes' walk away, in the same state that it left the kitchen. Because the patients are already ill, a hospital caterer has to ensure that the conditions under which the food is prepared are to a very high standard of hygiene. They will also be working under strict budgetary controls.

This is a senior management position and, although catering managers may have worked their way up from being chefs, with C&G or NVQ qualifications, others will have gained BTEC or degree qualifications and started as management trainees.

Housekeeper
This term is normally used in small institutions and covers all areas of domestic arrangements. See also page 27.

Hygienist
This job is usually found in hospitals, where a hygienist works closely with the catering manager to ensure that the conditions in which the food is prepared and served are as clean as possible. A hygienist may well have close links with the domestic services manager (see page 46) or work in an advisory capacity at several hospitals. They may also work directly for a local authority and give advice in all their public-sector establishments.

A hygienist will normally have BTEC or degree qualifications.

Kitchen porter
See page 27.

Linen-keeper
This job is a hugely important one in the hospital sector because of the vast quantities of linen used, and the sterilization processes that may be necessary to clean them. See also page 28.

Management trainee
See page 28.

Menu planner
This is another job title for a dish developer (see page 50) or diet chef (see page 46).

Nutritionist
This is an important job in any institution if it is providing all the inmates' food, such as in a children's home. It is closely related to the position of diet chef (see page 46), but a nutritionist is not a qualified chef and does not do any cooking. They concentrate on the content of the food provided to ensure that the nutritional balance is correct and make suggestions if there are deficiencies in the menu. They may also test new dishes, products (the various types of milk, say) or cooking methods (irradiation) as they come on the market to see how their use would affect the diets of the people within their care.

A nutritionist normally has BTEC or degree qualifications.

Personnel officer
See page 96.

Recruitment officer
See page 97.

Switchboard operator
Only larger institutions have switchboards. In many smaller establishments, the phone is answered by the administrative staff. See also page 99.

Storekeeper
See page 31.

Vegetable chef
See page 32.

Vegetarian chef
See page 32.

Waiter

This job is rarely found in the public sector. Many establishments operate self-service food areas that require only counter assistants and other domestic staff. In other establishments that have a plate service style of operation, the types of people being served necessitate the use of specialist administrative or auxiliary staff rather than waiters. Toddlers do not need waiters – they need someone to cut up their food and sometimes coax them to eat it; older people with arthritic hands may also need this type of assistance. Waiting staff may be found in some upmarket residential or sheltered accommodation for the elderly or in private hospitals. See also page 37.

Specialist employment

This heading covers those jobs that do not easily fall into other sectors and yet are part of the catering industry. Some of the jobs – such as those of butler and valet – are often considered to be archaic, yet they are alive, very well paid and eagerly sought after. These jobs are normally for people with an individualistic approach to life, who prefer to work for themselves or just one person rather than a company. Many of these jobs also involve periods of intensive work over long hours followed by periods of no work at all. Travel is often an attraction as well as a love of tradition.

The jobs

Butler

A butler does not usually work in the hotel sector, although they may be employed by a banqueting or conference centre from time to time. A butler usually works for a wealthy private family or royalty, supervising and hiring all domestic staff except in the housekeeping areas. They are expected to be on duty all the time the family is in residence, but, as such a family usually has several homes, there will be periods of days or weeks when the butler's time is their own. A butler will have special responsibility for the food and wine. Most butlers are privately trained at a school for butlers or will have been hotel assistants or general managers or footmen or stewards in one of the forces.

Demonstrator

This job is closely related to that of home economist (see page 94), but concentrates on customer contact and sales. The demonstrator will explain and show customers how a new piece of equipment or a new food product can be used and highlight its advantages. Often a demonstrator is freelance and may work either in the employer's showrooms or at exhibitions and so on.

Demonstrators are often paid on a commission basis and have NVQ or BTEC qualifications in Hospitality or Consumer Sciences.

Dish developer

A dish developer's job is often to refine classical dishes for mass production. Many companies that make complete meals employ dish developers. They are also employed to design dishes that take advantage of new technology and changing consumer tastes. Dish developers often work for companies that supply airlines with their food, such as Granada. Some may work for companies that also supply direct to the public, such as Marks & Spencer.

A dish developer will normally have a BTEC or degree qualification in Nutrition or Consumer Sciences.

Footman

This position can also be called junior butler. A footman performs many of the food service functions of a butler or of a highly skilled silver service waiter (see page 36) and of a sommelier (see page 37). They are normally employed by one of the large, wealthy, aristocratic households within the UK or overseas.

Footmen may well have NVQ and WSET qualifications and may train for a few months at a school for butlers in order to progress to the position of butler. See also page 49.

Master of ceremonies

They may also be called a toastmaster (see page 51).

Patissier

Besides working in the kitchens of large, high-class establishments, a patissier may often set up on their own and supply pastry goods to the trade. See also page 29.

Toastmaster

A toastmaster is often an ex-serviceman, normally someone who has served in the officers' mess (see mess steward, page 92). Toastmasters are hired for formal functions to announce grace, the speakers and propose the toasts. At very large functions, they may be used to marshal groups of people from one room to another.

Most toastmasters will have had some food service experience and belong to the Guild of Professional Toastmasters.

Valet

A valet may be employed by a five-star hotel or cruise liner or by a private individual. Their job in private service is to look after the clothes and personal possessions of their employer. This may range from starching evening dress to cleaning fishing tackle. Generally, a valet travels with their employer and may spend much time overseas. They may progress to butler (see page 49) after further training.

In an hotel, a valet will look after the guests' clothes, send clothes to the dry cleaners or clean them themselves where applicable. They will also do minor and emergency repairs. Many valets are ex-servicemen, probably batmen or mess stewards (see page 92) and some will become butlers.

The employers

The number of employers within the industry – not only in the UK but all over the world – is constantly increasing, and new hotels, leisure centres and theme parks are constantly being built. New jobs are being created all the time. Lists of employers can be obtained from the HCIMA, the *Caterer and Hotelkeeper*'s Annual Careers Supplement, from the reference sections of your local library and from the Internet. However, there are many self-employed people within the industry.

Twenty-five per cent of hotels within the UK are privately owned, so they will not be listed in the above places — just the large, national and international companies. However, jobs with all types of employer are advertised in local publications, such as the London *Evening Standard*, and national trade journals, such as the *Caterer and Hotelkeeper*, and certain special interest magazines, such as the Brewers' Society's magazine. There is also a number of specialist hotel and catering employment agencies that advertise regularly in the national press and can be found in the telephone directory.

Getting started

College courses – run on a full- or part-time basis – provide two ways of entry into the industry. Full-time courses over one, two or three years are often the most popular for school-leavers. Part-time courses are available for those who are already employed in the industry and looking to enhance their career prospects. Many people go into the industry without any qualifications and start at the bottom. In order to progress, however, most will gain some academic qualifications. See page 102 for information about which type of education establishment you should contact to gain suitable qualifications to progress your career.

If you want to go straight out to work – and many people do – you may want to contact your local TEC or Local Enterprise Council and find out about Modern Apprenticeship Schemes or National Training Certificates.

Pay

It is difficult to give an accurate guide to salaries. Casual and part-time staff are often paid by the hour and likely to be paid only the national minimum wage unless they have very specialist skills. Hotel front-office staff may earn anything from £12,000 to £18,000. Chefs are often paid anything from £10,000 to £30,000, depending on age, experience and position. A general manager of a large, international hotel may often be paid in excess of £60,000, with substantial perks. Someone working in the fast food restaurant sector may find themselves area manager by the time that they are 30 and earning £30,000 plus. If you own and run your own establishment, you will set your income limit yourself, depending on what the business earns. It should be noted, though, that allowances are not normally paid for working unsociable hours, such as weekends, as that is often part of the job. Overtime is only paid if excess hours or official bank holidays are worked.

Further information

See pages 124–37. For further information about the actual courses available, see page 102. Then, contact your local college or UCAS to see where they are run at the moment.

Chapter 2

Travel and tourism

'Tourism' is often described as involving travel arrangements, amenities and leisure activities. In this book, 'travel' has been defined as methods of travel, 'tourism' as the amenities at the destination and 'leisure' as sport and entertainment.

Anyone looking for employment within travel and tourism should be able to speak at least one other language. Within Europe, many choose to speak French, German or Spanish, while those hoping to follow a business career in Asia or the Pacific Rim would improve their chances by learning Japanese. However, if you intend to work in most foreign countries, another skill is often needed; for example, restaurant or bar work. These skills are often taught as part of an hotel/catering-based course and not as a major part of a travel industry course. For jobs in these sectors, see the relevant chapter.

Tourism

Tourism is one of the biggest growth industries in the United Kingdom, employing about 1½ million people, directly and indirectly, creating hundreds of new jobs each week, and contributing vast amounts to the wealth of the country.

The growth of tourism can be attributed to several factors. Improvements in methods of travel – such as faster planes, more luxurious trains and popular cruise lines – have made travelling much easier. Longer paid holidays have given people the opportunity to indulge in tourism as an accepted activity. Many people have a higher level of education and the urge to explore and experience new pursuits. Early retirement and occupational pensions have meant that there are many more elderly people who are fit, comfortably well off and keen to travel.

A tourist can be described as anyone who travels away from home, perhaps to enjoy the history and culture of a faraway city, to have a holiday, to learn a new language, perfect a sport or visit a country to seek medical attention. Tourists travel to the UK, within the UK and from the UK. The choice of jobs is thus extremely wide and expanding rapidly.

The jobs

In this chapter, all the jobs available in this area are mentioned, but only those with skills unique to travel and tourism are described in detail. Jobs also found in leisure but more relevant to that chapter will be fully described there to avoid duplication. Similarly, any jobs relating more to catering or the licensed trade are described in their relevant chapters.

Accounts
The day-to-day accounts will usually be recorded by senior members of staff who will then be able to pass the daily records to an accountant for completion. It is useful to have some knowledge of bookkeeping procedures and many NVQ courses will provide this to a basic level. See also page 91.

Amenity manager
See page 69.

Campsite manager
A campsite manager in the UK has a varied job because of the weather. In summer, they are responsible for the general care and maintenance of a holiday camp site, including all facilities. This will include showers and toilets, restaurants and snack bars, a licensed bar, swimming pools, adventure playgrounds and any other form of entertainment, as well as the general running of the camp site. The winter is often spent maintaining, repairing and redecorating public areas.

A BTEC qualification and experience within a service industry are an advantage.

Caravan park manager

This position is similar to that of camp site manager. While many people bring their own caravans on to the site, there are also caravans for hire. During the closed season, these often have to be maintained in addition to the public areas.

Although many camp sites are privately owned, it is recommended that people entering this sector of the industry have relevant HE qualifications in a management discipline.

Cashier

See page 23.

Conference organizer

Within the travel, tourism and leisure industry, a conference organizer is often a specialist, organizing conferences and packages within a specific area. A conference organizer can also be found in an hotel. See also page 24.

Courier

A courier is based at a holiday resort such as Playa de Las Americas, Tenerife or at a business destination. Greeting and meeting the travellers is part of the job, as well as advising on local traditions and customs, selling tours and excursions, and sorting out problems in the resort. Couriers may accompany groups on excursions, and will have to give information about the locality, such as the history of a local church and the times of church services. They will also have to converse in the language of the country. The job is exhausting, and needs patience, tact, diplomacy, plus a party spirit if dealing with holidaymakers. However, this is also a most satisfying area to work in.

NVQ and GNVQ qualifications are a good basis from which to start.

Curator

See Museum management, page 58.

Guest services

See page 26.

Guide

A guide may be found at an attraction (for example, the Tower of London) or giving tourists a guided tour of an area, city or town, such as Stratford-upon-Avon or Sheffield. Many guides are fluent in several languages, dealing with tourists from all over the world. Many guides work freelance and the most highly qualified are employed all year round.

Qualifications in travel and tourism are often essential, and guides must be extremely knowledgeable about the area in which they are employed. An outgoing personality and the ability to speak in public are also essential.

Heritage centre personnel

A heritage centre is more than just a stately home, castle or previous home of someone famous. Increasingly nowadays, a traditional heritage centre has a safari park, vintage cars or something similar to offer. It can be described as a combination of a stately home and a leisure park, entertainment for all the family, and is often run along these lines.

There are also increasing numbers of industrial heritage centres. These tend to be the sites of old factories, woollen mills, potteries and so on and are visited both by ordinary tourists and educational groups wanting to learn about the past.

Many of the jobs are similar to jobs in other areas, so see under the appropriate headings. However, in an industrial heritage centre, personnel would also be expected to know about the original function of the site and may even be required to demonstrate how machinery used to work!

Holiday centre staff

Working at a holiday centre is rather like working at an hotel in a holiday resort. Jobs are often similar, providing food, accommodation and entertainment for holidaymakers. Some holiday centres have a specialism, such as sports facilities, dealing with small children or helping the handicapped. For further details, see the specific job you are interested in, such as chef (page 24), receptionist (page 30) or Redcoat (page 58).

Human Resources manager

See page 95.

Licensee
See page 85.

Management trainee
College-leavers with good BTEC or higher education qualifications are not usually given managerial positions immediately. They generally undergo a company training scheme lasting between 6 and 12 months in the specialism they have chosen to enable them to gain hands-on experience and fill any practical gaps in their knowledge. At the end of the training period, they are normally given a supervisory or junior management position.

Museum management
A museum manager or curator is someone who organizes the exhibits in a museum or gallery. Often a curator or manager has the authority to purchase and borrow exhibits within rigid budgetary controls.

Responsible for daily administration, the job needs high-level qualifications, such as a HND and/or degree, in a relevant specialism, in addition to service industry experience.

Public relations
See page 96.

Purser
This is a similar post to an hotel manager (see page 26), although a purser is employed on board commercial, passenger-carrying ships. They therefore have to ensure that all the necessary pre-planning is carried out, as replenishment of stocks may be difficult during certain parts of a voyage, such as mid Atlantic.

Receptionist
See page 30.

Recruitment officer
See page 97.

Redcoat
A holiday centre provides food, accommodation and entertainment. There may be specialist activities, such as pony trekking or water sports. The Redcoats, who are often seasonal employees, organize facilities and entertainment for those on holiday. These

may include a children's party, a wet T-shirt competition, water aerobics or an old time music hall.

Redcoats always need an outgoing personality as well as NVQ or GNVQ qualifications in a relevant field. In addition to service industry experience, many have worked in a sports centre or entertainments complex.

Resort publicity officer

The role of a resort publicity officer combines much of the work of the tourist boards and the tourist information centres. Responsible for the promotion of a town, such as Brighton, Blackpool or Bradford, a resort publicity officer will try to find ways to highlight certain attractions and the resort in its entirety. For example, Brighton for the Lanes and Royal Pavilion, Blackpool for the lights and Bradford for the industrial history visible there.

BTEC, degree or postgraduate qualifications in tourism, together with employment experience with a tourist board or tourist information centre, are essential.

Sales and marketing
See page 98.

Stately home guide
See Guide, page 57.

Switchboard
See Telephonist, page 99.

Tour operator
See page 64.

Tour representative
See Courier, page 56.

Tourist board staff

The Development of Tourism Act 1969 created four national tourist boards – the British Tourist Authority (BTA), English Tourist Board, Scottish Tourist Board and Welsh Tourist Board. In addition to promoting the development of tourism, facilities and attractions in Great Britain, the national tourist boards have the authority to publicize an area, advise and inform, research and provide valuable financial assistance for tourism-related projects. For instance, the main role of the BTA is to promote incoming tourism to Britain with the help of its overseas offices.

As an employee of a tourist board, you are likely to have a clerical position, dealing with educational trips, promotions, or assisting with queries. A BTEC qualification in tourism is essential.

Tourist information centre staff

An information centre provides tourists with information, maps, lists of local attractions and tours, times of buses and trains, and much more. There are over 700 information centres in the United Kingdom; some are seasonal and others open all year round. Their main job is dealing with the public, giving advice, liaising with local attractions and hotels, and selling maps, post cards and information guides.

NVQ qualifications are an ideal entry into the business.

Yellowcoat

See Redcoat, page 58.

Travel

The travel industry covers a broad area, including making reservations, organizing tickets, confirming holiday accommodation, in addition to providing the means of transport, whether it is by ship, plane, train, coach or other more adventurous methods, such as camel trekking in the Australian outback.

Much of the work of someone in the travel industry is within the United Kingdom, although many jobs involve travel for the employee as well, not just the customer. People don't always travel for holidays; some travel a long way to get to work; some travel for their education; some travel for business reasons; some buy through a travel agent a complete package to receive medical attention.

Package tours are popular with many holidaymakers who want a deal that will include all the travel arrangements, accommodation and many other features, such as tours. These holidays are put together by a tour operator. However, arrangements can also be made via a travel agent just to reserve accommodation or buy tickets or to put together an individual package.

Several employers within the industry are known nationally and internationally, such as British Airways, Virgin, Cathay Pacific, United Airlines, Thomas Cook, Princess Cruises.

The career tree on page 123 gives good examples of how you can work in travel and move from one area of the industry to another.

The jobs

The world of travel makes one think of dashing around the globe, meeting people. This can be true, although there are many other aspects of equal importance within the industry, such as the travel agents who sell, tour operators who create packages, transport staff who assist the travellers. Many people choose to enter the travel industry because they feel that it will enable them to travel the world and, clearly, one of the perks will be the chance to travel to many exotic and interesting destinations, but it should be remembered that many jobs are UK-based.

The jobs listed below are all found within the industry and will enable you to choose a suitable career path.

Accounts
The day-to-day accounts records will normally be kept by the senior members of staff, who will then be able to pass the daily records to an accountant for completion.

It is useful to have some knowledge of bookkeeping procedures and many NVQ courses will include this to a basic level.

Air cabin crew
Cabin crew are responsible for their passengers from the time they board the plane until the time it reaches its destination. Tasks include the serving of food and beverages, sale of duty-free products and general care of all passengers.

Airline personnel are trained to deal with emergencies, including first aid and problem passengers. Flights can be very different one from the other, varying in length from 30 minutes to 15 hours, to a hot climate or a cold climate, be on large planes such as a DC10 or Boeing 747, or a small commuter plane, perhaps from London to Edinburgh.

It is important that you are able to communicate effectively and politely, for long periods, and look smart at all times – even after a long-haul flight when you are tired. Most of the recognized airlines will only recruit those aged 21 or over, and often prefer candidates to have experience within the service industry, such as an hotel or restaurant background. In addition, it helps if you have a good knowledge of a foreign language. NVQ and GNVQ qualifications in a relevant discipline will enable you to gain the necessary experience.

Cashier
See page 23.

Client services manager
See Guest services, page 26.

Cruise operator
A cruise operator, such as P&O, sells packages to those who prefer to sail and enjoy several ports of call and have a series of destinations rather than fly directly to just one place.

Cruise operators can be regarded as specialist travel agents (see page 64) who assemble holiday packages in a very specific area. What is included in any one package varies, depending on the market it is aimed at and the destinations. For example, a three-month luxury cruise, an educational trip to the 'Roman ports' of the Mediterranean or one week observing the wildlife of the Arctic will be quite different from each other.

Working for a cruise operator involves being either an administrator or a member of the seagoing staff. A cruise liner is like a floating hotel with all the facilities and luxuries you expect of a high-class hotel.

NVQ and/or GNVQ/BTEC qualifications in a related field are an ideal entrance to this area of the travel industry.

Ground steward
A ground steward is employed by an airline. The work includes the selling and issuing of tickets, the checking in of passengers prior to their flights and guiding and assisting travellers with any problems at the airport.

NVQ, BTEC or travel management qualification in ticketing is an advantage in addition to appropriate service industry or reception experience.

Hotel booking agency
An hotel booking agency is often found at entry points for travellers, such as mainline railway stations, airports, sea ports and city centres. An agency will have detailed knowledge of hotels in the area, selling accommodation and facilities.

NVQ or BTEC qualifications are needed in addition to some reservations experience in hotels.

Human resources manager
See page 95.

Management trainee
See page 58.

Public relations
See page 96.

Receptionist
See page 30.

Recruitment
See page 97.

Reservations clerk
A reservations clerk will deal with travel arrangements and holidays for clients. See also Travel agent, page 64.

Resort representative
See Courier, page 56.

Steward
A steward may be found on board ship, on an intercity train or with an airline. See also Air cabin crew (page 61), Waiter (page 37) and Armed forces (pages 92 and 98).

Tour manager
See Courier, page 56.

Tour operator

A tour operator prepares holiday packages that can be sold to the public directly or through a travel agent. These include trips to popular holiday resorts, such as the Algarve in Portugal, Disneyland in Florida, or specialist holidays, such as a walking tour in Nepal.

Working for a tour operator may involve planning a package trip, preparing a brochure, selling the holidays or undertaking administrative tasks. One of the perks is the opportunity to travel at discounted rates.

A good qualification, such as NVQ or BTEC, is an excellent way to start a career in tour operations.

Tour representative

See Courier, page 56.

Travel agent

The main task of a travel agent is to either arrange transport and accommodation or sell all-inclusive holidays to travellers. The job also includes the arranging of day trips, skiing holidays and perhaps the booking of theatre tickets.

A good travel agent will know how to use timetables for ferries, buses and trains, and be familiar with airlines and airports worldwide. In addition, they must be able to complete tickets, and use computer systems such as Travicom. Some agents specialize in travel to certain destinations, others in business travel and some have facilities for the traveller to buy foreign currency. One of the obvious perks of the job is the possibility of reduced-rate travel. Most travel agents just starting in the industry have NVQ qualifications or a BTEC in Travel and Tourism.

The employers

The rapid growth of the travel and tourism industry has brought with it a number of new employers, all wishing to participate in the ever-increasing market. Many choose to specialize in a certain area, such as South America, safaris or the business market. This has meant that new jobs have been created and are advertised in national publications, such as the *Travel Trade Gazette*, and local papers, such as the London *Evening Standard*. Among the employers are airlines, such as British Airways, Britannia, Virgin or Ryan Air, shipping lines, such as Princess Cruises and P&O, coach services, such as National Express or Stagecoach, travel agents and tour operators, including Thomas Cook, Flying Colours, Lunn Poly, Going Places and Cosmos. Those wishing to pursue a career in tourism can look to tourist boards, tourist attractions or resorts for possible employment.

Getting started

College courses are run on a full-time or part-time basis for all areas of the travel and tourism industry. School-leavers may find that full-time courses are more beneficial as they often include a period of work experience. Part-time courses are popular with those already employed in the industry who hope to gain further qualifications. Some people may also choose to follow a MAp or NTC scheme.

Once you have obtained academic qualifications, it is possible to choose which type of employer you would like to work for – airline, tour operator, travel agent, tourist board and so on. Many people who hope to work for an airline find that they need to be over a certain age – often 21. Until they can apply, as a starting point, many work in a related area, such as a service industry, where meeting the public is important, and acquire some basic NVQ qualifications that will stand them in good stead later on in their chosen profession.

Personal qualities

Any career that involves working as part of a team and dealing with members of the public calls for an enthusiastic, hard-working, bright, conscientious person with an outgoing personality and the ability to work long and often unsociable hours under pressure. Many people within the industry have succeeded not because of their qualifications, but because of their personality, which enables them to cope with different, often trying situations.

Pay

Authority, responsibility and experience are some of the most important factors when assessing pay. Thus, a trainee travel agent may start on £7000 per year, while the owner of the travel agency may be earning £50,000. It is difficult to give accurate information as there are many jobs with different employers in varying areas within the industry. Those people who have higher qualifications may enter the industry at a more senior level, and those who choose to work for local authorities or large companies may have a structured career and pay scale; cabin crew may be paid a bonus on sales, a guide is often self-employed, a camp site manager can earn as much as a hotel manager, assuming that the camp stays open all year. As in many other industries, staff paid weekly often receive extra payments for overtime and allowances, while salaried staff may be part of a profit-sharing scheme or be given bonuses or regional weightings. It should be noted, however, that in many areas of the industry, unsociable hours are part of the job and do not necessarily count towards extra payments.

Equal opportunities

The travel and tourism industry is an equal opportunities employer with many ethnic minorities encouraged to participate because of their specialist knowledge. However, equal status work is not always easy to find in some countries where there may be active sex discrimination and some covert racial discrimination. Before accepting an overseas position, it would be wise to check out local customs and practices with the relevant high commission or embassy.

Union membership

Union membership is usually only significant among airline staff and those in public service.

Within the private sector, many large companies have staff associations. Representatives of all grades of staff sit on these associations and help to solve problems that arise and transmit information from top management to the staff for feedback, perhaps when a new company policy is being considered, for example. Representatives will be called on for discussions on pay increases and any matters that may affect staff.

Many agencies belong to a professional body, such as ABTA or IATA.

Entry requirements and training

Many people enter the travel and tourism industry with few, if any, qualifications. However, an increasing market of qualified people has meant that competition is much fiercer than previously. Colleges all over the country run courses for part-time and full-time students who wish to enter the industry, all supported by NVQ, the Academy of Travel Management, BTEC and the ABTA National Training Board.

Many colleges offer their own diploma, a package of essential subjects for those entering the industry, including information technology, communication studies and handling financial transactions. If you decide to take a college diploma, you should ensure that nationally recognized subjects are taught by checking with any of the relevant professional associations.

Further information

See pages 124–37. For further information about the actual courses available, see page 102. Then, contact your local college or UCAS to see where they are run at the moment.

Chapter 3
Leisure

The leisure industry is clearly one of the fastest-growing sectors in the world today. Ever-increasing leisure time has meant that new kinds of activities are being made popular, such as ice skating, ice hockey and quasar games. Thus, new jobs are being created all the time.

Non-sporting leisure

It would be quite impossible to describe the complete range of activities available during leisure time. The choice is enormous, from visiting bars to nightclubs, from bingo halls to cinemas, concerts or an entertainment complex. Additionally, there are hobbies and pastimes, such as line-dancing, amateur dramatics or photography, giving a wide and varied choice. One thing that can be said, however, is that people's leisure time is increasing, and with it their desire to experience much more.

The jobs

The leisure industry offers a tremendous range of careers, using numerous skills. In the past, the industry has been flexible in its approach to recruitment, looking for enthusiasm and personal qualities alone. However, fierce competition for jobs has made qualifications more important in today's growing industry, leading to an increase in the courses and qualifications available, and to employers' expectations that applicants will have some form of academic qualification.

The jobs described below cover a sample of those available in the leisure industry. Many jobs are interchangeable or are given a different title within another chapter or section. For example, the licensee of a bar in a leisure or entertainment complex is no different from a licensee at a holiday camp. For this reason, only those jobs that are unique to the leisure sector have been described here, with cross-references being given for those jobs described elsewhere.

Accounts
See page 91.

Amenity manager
An amenity manager is responsible for the daily organization of a recreational or social centre, an art gallery, a swimming pool, amusement park or leisure centre. Dealing with the public on a daily basis is an important aspect of an amenity manager's job, which also includes managing staff, catering outlets and the general management of an attraction.

Entry requirements will vary according to the specialism involved, although BTEC or degree qualifications are a good introduction, followed by employment in the industry.

Cashier
See page 34.

Conference organizer
See page 41.

Cruise operator
See page 62.

Doorstaff
Another rather old-fashioned name for the doorstaff is bouncer. It is the responsibility of doorstaff to ensure that dress codes are enforced, people unfit to enter the establishment – because they are drunk or violent, say – are not admitted, to calm down the situation when celebrations start to get out of hand and eject those who won't behave in a peaceful, law-abiding manner.

Although most doorstaff have no qualifications when they begin, those wanting to work in high-class establishments or make a career on the security side of the industry will take relevant NVQ qualifications; many are also qualified first aiders.

Entertainment centre manager

An entertainment centre is a leisure centre, theatre and restaurant all rolled into one.

The jobs involved are numerous and are to be found under their relevant headings. The managerial positions closely resemble that of a hotel manager, and involve personnel, food and beverage service, licensee duties, guest relations and so on.

Experience within hotels, restaurants and the world of entertainment, together with a recognized qualification, are essential.

Holiday camp manager

A holiday camp is similar to a hotel that caters mainly for holidaymakers. The guests are keen to enjoy themselves and the management must ensure that they do. Many of the jobs are the same as in a hotel, with receptionists taking reservations and checking people in, room or chalet attendants taking care of accommodation and cleaning, catering personnel in the restaurant and kitchen and entertainers during the day and evening.

A manager of a camp has overall control and is responsible for its day-to-day running. They are accountable to the guests to ensure that they have an enjoyable time, to the employees for their welfare and to the owners for profits.

Most people entering this area of work will have taken HE qualifications and started as a management trainee (see page 28).

Human resources manager

See page 95.

Leisure park staff

While the majority of jobs are similar to those found in a theme park, entertainment centre or holiday camp, there are many jobs open to specialists. For example, teachers in activities such as horseriding, water sports, climbing, mountaineering and so on, are often required.

Licensee

See page 85.

Management trainee
Many college-leavers with BTEC or degree qualifications in a relevant area begin their career as a supervisor or management trainee. See also pages 28 and 58.

Nightclub manager
As a thorough knowledge of licensing law is required by all nightclub managers, see Chapter 4, The licensed trade, page 79, for further information.

Public relations officer
See page 96.

Purser
See page 58.

Receptionist
A receptionist in a leisure centre is similar to a receptionist in many other areas. The role involves responsibility for many of the office practices, including the handling of visitor enquiries, cash handling and reservations. See also pages 23 and 30.

Redcoat
See page 58.

Sales and marketing
See page 98.

Social events organizer
A social events organizer often does not work in the hospitality industry directly. They may work for a large international company such as British Petroleum and organize, on behalf of senior management, a wide variety of functions. This may include overseas conferences, Christmas parties, dinner parties for visiting dignitaries, social programmes and excursions for their partners if they are accompanied. It is important for the organizer to be aware of different events in the location and areas of interest, in addition to accommodation. The individual appointed as social events organizer has to be prepared to work long and sometimes unsociable hours, especially while the event is taking place.

BTEC or degree qualifications are the normal entry criteria and knowledge of the industry, business management and self-motivation are important.

Switchboard operator
See telephonist, page 99.

Telephonist
See page 99.

Theme park manager
Again, this role is very similar to that of an hotel manager, but with additional responsibility for the attractions. Accommodation may or may not be included.

Theme park staff
A theme park, such as Legoland or Alton Towers, provides family entertainment – activities and rides, things to do and things to see, places to drink and eat – for people of all ages. There are various jobs, many of which will be found under another heading. For example, cashiers are needed at the point of entry, information centre staff throughout and food and beverage service staff in refreshment areas. Other specialist staff, including gardeners, maintenance or security, although essential, are specialists within their particular area and so you will need to research these yourself.

Yellowcoat
See Redcoat, page 58.

Sport

The importance of staying fit, eating well and generally caring for ourselves, together with more leisure time, has brought about the rise in popularity of sports centres, which are those with two or more main sports facilities. Recreation is an area that has expanded rapidly during the last 30 years, culminating in over 1000 local authority-run sports centres in Britain today, along with many more privately run sports clubs and centres. Together with the traditional sports of football, tennis, swimming, hockey and squash, sports centres are now likely to offer many of the following: weight training, aerobics, stretch and dance classes, fencing, saunas and spas, sailing and canoeing, volleyball, ice skating, roller skating, climbing walls. Many offer additional services such as physiotherapy, massage and aromatherapy. The increase in popularity of sport as recreation has also turned the sports centre into a social environment with people using it as a meeting point. Some sports centres are within an hotel, many are privately owned and others are administered by a local authority.

The jobs

The demand for sports centres with a range of facilities and the fact that they are now seen as social meeting places have increased the variety and number of jobs available. Indeed, there are several sports centres in the UK with total annual admissions of over 1 million people, and many others that deal with over 500, 000 customers each year.

The number of admissions is a useful guide in assessing the scale and scope of the management required within a centre. Many sports centres offer restaurant and catering facilities, most have reservation systems, many hire out equipment and most run classes and have qualified teachers on site to teach those interested how to participate in their chosen sport. What a particular centre offers clearly influences the jobs available there. Specialist jobs, such as a diving instructor at a swimming pool, a judo or football coach, have not been included in the list of jobs for obvious reasons, but you will find jobs that are essential for the daily organization and administration of a leisure or sports centre. Many of the jobs are similar to those found in other areas, so, to avoid duplication, they have not been described, but, rather, are cross-referenced. It must be noted that all employees should be actively interested in sport.

Accounts
See page 91.

Cashier
One of the tasks of a cashier in a leisure centre is the hiring out of sports equipment after the receipt of a deposit or other form of

security. Sports centres will usually charge admission, and the cashier is responsible for issuing entrance tickets and reconciling cash received. Many establishments are also clubs and have various forms of membership, such as full membership, family rates or limited access rates. The cashier will often be responsible for membership sales and acknowledging receipt of fees, and perform the duties of a receptionist. If the centre has a catering facility, a cashier may be employed in this area. See also page 23, and Receptionist, page 30.

Holiday camp manager
See page 70.

Human resources manager
See page 95.

Leisure centre assistant
The job of a leisure centre assistant will vary according to the type of establishment. For example, it may be a sports centre or an entertainment centre. Those employed in sporting activities may be called on to act as supervisors, lifeguards or coaches. At other times, they perform clerical duties, such as issuing equipment or reserving tennis and squash courts.

It is important to be physically fit and keen on all sports. NVQ or BTEC qualifications are usually the entry-level requirement.

Leisure centre manager
In many ways, a manager of a leisure or sports centre has transferable skills and a unique specialism. Day-to-day organization of staff, catering for members of the public, administration and managerial techniques are similar to those found in many other management positions.

A degree in sports studies or recreation management or a BTEC qualification in leisure studies are ideal methods of entry into the industry as they combine the specialisms of a sporting environment with the necessary business studies.

Leisure park staff
See page 70.

Management trainee
See page 28.

Personal trainer
Many leisure clubs provide personal trainers for people who have specific health problems or prefer to work on a one-to-one basis rather than in a class.

Personal trainers need to have good social skills as well as an NVQ or BTEC in sports and recreation.

Public relations
See page 96.

Receptionist
It is important for receptionists to show an active interest in all aspects of sport. This position will often combine the usual aspects of the role with those of a cashier. See also page 30.

Recreation assistant
See Leisure centre assistant, page 74.

Recruitment officer
See page 97.

Sales and marketing
See page 98.

Sports centre staff
This group covers all the roles in a sports centre, from manager to cashier, waiter to sales personnel, so see the area of interest.

Telephonist
See page 99.

The employers

Employers can be found in both the private and public sectors – that is, local authority parks and sports centres or private theatres and clubs. Lists of large national and international employers (for example, Granada Leisure, Metropolitan or David Lloyd

Clubs) can be obtained from *Leisure Management* or the reference section of your local library.

Jobs with all types of employer are advertised in publications such as *Leisure Opportunities* and local papers like the London *Evening Standard*, and *Opportunities for Work* advertises jobs with local authorities. Some jobs, such as food production staff within a leisure centre, are advertised in the magazines for related areas (for example, the *Caterer and Hotelkeeper*). There are also a number of employment agencies that advertise regularly in the national press and can be found in the telephone directory.

Getting started

College courses are run on a full-time or part-time basis for all areas of the leisure industry. School-leavers sometimes find that full-time courses are more beneficial as they often include a period of work experience. Part-time courses are more popular with those already employed in the industry who hope to gain further qualifications.

Once you have college certificates and some work experience, it is possible to choose which type of employer you wish to work for (for example, public or private sector). Those wanting a career in a sports-related area may find it easier to approach local authorities for employment in parks, leisure centres and sports clubs before pursuing a job with a privately run sports complex. For those wanting a non-sporting leisure career, there are many entertainment, activity or holiday centres constantly seeking people to join an ambitious, conscientious, hard-working team, such as the Disney Corporation.

Personal qualities

Whichever area of leisure you choose to follow as a career, you need to be an enthusiastic, bright, lively person who can work as part of a team and perform well under pressure. For example, after a long day, a sports centre assistant may be asked to coach a group of people who appear to be untalented in a certain area. It would be easy to become lazy and uninterested. A holidaymaker may continually complain, always unsatisfied with something. It is vital to have the necessary social skills to be able to deal with all kinds of people. Personality is important and many who have succeeded have done so not because of their academic qualifications, but through their ability to work in a service industry.

Pay

It is difficult to give any accurate information on pay. Obviously, the level of responsibility is an important factor when comparing the pay for one job with that for another. A leisure centre manager may earn somewhere in the region of £16,000–£25,000 per year, depending on the size of the complex. A pool attendant may earn only £4.50 per hour, while other sports centre staff may earn anything from £150 per week upwards, depending on the positions they hold. Those who coach a specialized sport may be able to command a higher level of pay. A holiday camp manager will often be paid on a similar scale to a hotel manager. Pay will also vary from one company to another as will the perks. Many salaried staff may earn much more than their basic pay because of a profit-sharing scheme, bonuses and regional weightings. Staff paid weekly may receive overtime, bonuses and allowances in addition to their basic pay.

Equal opportunities

The leisure industry is an equal opportunities employer, with an equal number of men and women, and many members of ethnic minority groups holding top jobs. Legislation has, however, allowed discrimination in certain jobs, such as in an all-female health club. However, in general, all jobs are open to male and female applicants.

Union membership

There are few union members within the industry except in the public sector, such as for local authority sports centres, amenities and attractions. Those wishing to belong to a union may join the GMWU.

Managerial staff often prefer to join a professional body, such as the Institute of Leisure and Amenity Management or Royal Society of Health. The Institute represents professionals in all areas of leisure, both sporting and non-sporting.

Entry requirements and training

Courses tend to divide into the sporting and non-sporting. For instance, there are courses at various levels entitled Sport and Leisure, and Recreation and Leisure awarded by NVQ, BTEC and at degree level. Most courses have business studies elements and are aimed at the industry as a whole, not just at the sportsperson. Consequently, those choosing such a course should realize that progression to a managerial or supervisory level will involve acquiring knowledge of financial and personnel management and that many of the courses will cover these areas.

The industry is changing rapidly and, although it is possible to enter it with basic NVQ qualifications, progression and promotion may only be possible for those with recognized certification at an appropriate level. Courses are available on a full-time, part-time or day-release basis.

Further information

See pages 124–37. For further information about the actual courses available, see page 102. Then contact your local college or UCAS to see where they are run at the moment.

Chapter 4
The licensed trade

What the term includes

The term 'licensed trade' covers a much wider variety of outlets than is often considered – pubs, wine bars, café bars, cocktail bars, clubs and so on. Some establishments are independently owned. In the case of a pub, for instance, this would be a 'free house', meaning it is not attached to a parent company. Other establishments are owned by large, multinational chains, such as Bass or Whitbread, and yet others by smaller, specialist chains, such as Eldridge Pope or Davy's Wine Bars. Some establishments may have just one room, while others may have several different areas for different customers — that is, an area for eating, an area for children, public bar, lounge bar and so on.

The vast majority of people start work in the licensed trade serving behind a bar. They may progress to cellar work and then move on to management. Some people work towards owning their own establishment, while others prefer to work for a large chain. Most people will work in several sectors before they decide which area suits them best.

It should be noted that while pubs are fairly easy to define, there are many different kinds of bars, and the types of bars described in this chapter are not definitive. However, the types of bars described do cover the major sectors and most other bar styles are a merger of one or more of the styles described or a variation on a traditional pub theme.

Pubs

Pubs are those establishments the primary purpose of which is the sale of alcoholic and non-alcoholic beverages. Typically, pubs are known for the beers and lagers they sell. They also usually have high spirit sales. Some pubs will specialize in 'real ales' – that is, traditional cask ales – and may be connected to a microbrewery. Others will specialize in keg and bottled beers. Many of them sell food, too. Many of these establishments are owned by the large brewing companies and may belong to a chain such as Inntrepreneur. Some pubs, mainly the chains, also have themes, such as the Wetherspoon chain, or they may follow the current fashion, which at the moment is either for Irish pubs or 'traditional' spit 'n' sawdust pubs. Many pubs, especially in small town or rural locations, form an integral part of the community.

Wine bars

Wine bars specialize in selling wines. Sometimes they sell other alcoholic beverages, such as spirits or premium beers, but some will choose to sell only wines and have restricted liquor licences to that effect. All wine bars will also sell non-alcoholic beverages and they usually sell food as well. Some wine bars also have a wholesale business attached and sell wines by the case.

Unlike pubs, which can be found in all locations, wine bars are usually to be found in urban areas where the customer base has a fairly high disposable income. Some wine bars are independently owned, but many are part of a chain, such as Yates Wine Lodges.

Café bars

Café bars could be said to be a combination of a wine bar and a Continental café. A range of alcoholic and non-alcoholic beverages will be available, including probably a range of speciality coffees and perhaps teas. There will also be a small range of cocktails, snacks and light meals. Therefore, customers can have a cup of coffee and read their paper; share a bottle of wine with friends; have a meal; or all three.

Café bars usually have children's certificates and so, like a Continental café and unlike a conventional restaurant, an adult can have an apéritif, while a child has an ice-cream – there is no need to have a full meal. Café bars are often independently owned or may be part of a chain, such as Greenalls Cellars.

Cocktail Bar

Cocktail bars can either be found as a standalone establishment or, more often, as an integral part of a restaurant complex.

The purpose of cocktail bars is to provide a wide range of mixed drinks, either alcoholic or non-alcoholic. They would normally have a limited range of wines, few or no draught beers, but a wide range of premium bottled beers.

Cocktail bars do not usually serve any food other than appetizers. Generally, a cocktail bar is part of a restaurant, as in TGI Fridays or Planet Hollywood, and customers will come to the bar for a few drinks before going on to have a meal. During their meal, waiters may collect drinks from the bar for the customers or drinks may come from the restaurant's own dispense bar.

In an hotel, guests of the hotel may use its cocktail bar as a social meeting place, having a drink before or after going somewhere outside the hotel.

There are a few cocktail bars that are not part of an hotel or restaurant, where people go just to spend the night drinking cocktails. In this case, they are likely to serve light meals as well as appetizers.

Clubs

There are many kinds of clubs. In private members' clubs, the members themselves will decide what style of bar the establishment will have. More usually, commercial clubs, such as nightclubs, will have several bars within the one establishment, where a large range of alcoholic and non-alcoholic beverages will be sold. Occasionally, one of the bars may have a specialist theme – such as cocktails only or wines only – but generally there is no specialization. As the main purpose of a nightclub is to dance, most of the drinks sold will be long, cold and fashionable, such as pre-bottled mixed beverages. Not all nightclubs are open every day of the week, but when they are open, the hours of work can be very long.

Some nightclubs are independently owned, others may be part of a group, such as Virgin or Bass, others may be part of a club-based group, such as the Peter Stringfellow Organization.

The jobs

Everyone who works with alcohol must be 18 or over. This does not mean that everyone who works in a pub, for instance, is over 18. A cleaner or glass collector could be younger or the employee could be participating in an authorized training scheme, such as a Modern Apprenticeship. The age limit is a legal requirement throughout the United Kingdom and so most employers will not be interested in considering anyone under 18 for any type of employment in case they accidentally become involved in the provision of alcoholic beverages.

People under 18 who want to enter this sector are usually advised to take a full-time course in a related area, such as an Advanced-level Hospitality and Catering GNVQ, so that they can gain relevant qualifications while waiting to reach an age at which they can be legally employed. This type of qualification is also very useful because many of these outlets are also found as part of other establishments. For instance, most hotels will have a bar of some kind and, conversely, many pubs now also make a large part of their income from the sale of food, many have function rooms and a few have bedrooms. Leisure complexes can often have a pub, a cocktail bar and a nightclub on the same site.

As a result of this overlap, the jobs described in this section are those that are directly related to the licensed trade. Those jobs that are more commonly found in other disciplines – such as chef – are cross-referenced rather than described here. Unlike the other chapters, all the jobs are listed together as one block. This is because many of the functions – such as licensee or bartender – apply to all jobs in this sector. You will have to use your common sense in deciding which jobs apply only to specific parts of this sector – for example, specialist cellar skills are only required where draught beer is sold – and which jobs are applicable across the board. Note that where the establishment is independently owned, the owner will often undertake all jobs anyway, as well as hiring other skilled or semi-skilled staff.

Accounts
See page 91.

Area manager
See page 92.

Bar manager
A bar manager is in charge of one or more bars within the same establishment. They are responsible for the staff and their behaviour, the supply of drinks and their control, the equipment within the bars; they are also financially accountable for this department. A bar manager may also work in an exhibition or conference centre, a nightclub, holiday camp and so on.

A bar manager will always have had experience as a bartender and usually have BTEC/GNVQ and BII qualifications.

Bartender
A bartender is normally unqualified unless they work in a cocktail bar, when they would have NVQ qualifications. They may work in many different kinds of establishment, such as pubs, conference centres, hotels, holiday camps and so on.

They are responsible for the serving of all alcoholic beverages and many soft drinks, often including coffee. A bartender must have a good working knowledge of the liquor licensing laws, be able to handle cash and work under extreme pressure.

A bartender may be working for NVQ, BTEC and/or BII qualifications in order to progress.

Brewer
A brewer is a person who brews or makes their own beer. In this context, the name does not apply to the employees of national brewing companies. Most brewers either own or have the tenancy of a pub and use this as the main outlet for their products.

They are often unqualified, but may have, or be working for, NVQ or BTEC qualifications. They may have worked previously for one of the large brewing chains, but are usually self-employed or in a limited form of partnership. They are also likely to have BII qualifications.

Cashier
Cashiers are generally found in clubs within the licensed trade, and it is often a job that is combined with those of receptionist and telephonist. See pages 23 and 99.

Cellar person
A cellar person is normally employed in a large establishment that has several bars, such as a large hotel, large pub, wine bar, conference centre or nightclub.

Their job is to receive deliveries of alcoholic and non-alcoholic drinks, make sure that they are stored correctly and securely, distribute the various drinks to the different bars on request and collect and return empty containers, such as beer kegs and various bottles, to the suppliers.

A cellar person is usually unqualified and may take NVQ or BII qualifications in order to progress.

Chef
See page 24.

Cocktail person
A cocktail person is someone who works in a cocktail bar and has alcoholic beverage qualifications, which ensure that they have the ability and knowledge to make many different cocktails on request. They must also be able to manage a high-class spirits bar.

Personality is important for this job, along with a high level of skills. A cocktail bar person would normally also hold NVQ and perhaps BII qualifications. A cocktail person may progress to bar manager, and may well be a member of the UK Bartenders Guild.

Doorstaff
Unfortunately, as a result of problems with violence or other unacceptable behaviour that can be associated with excessive alcohol consumption, and drug usage in some clubs, some establishments have to employ doorstaff to ensure harmony and compliance with the law in their establishments. For further details, see page 69.

Freetrader
A freetrader is a particular type of licensee (see below). Unlike a licensee, a freetrader can buy their alcohol from any supplier they

choose and so is not 'tied' to the company that owns the establishment.

Most licensees outside the pub trade are freetraders, but the majority within it are 'tied' to the brewery that owns their pub and must buy their supplies via that company.

A 'free house' pub will be owned by a freetrader, usually on a freehold basis, which usually means that there is a much wider range of drinks available than in a 'tied' house. Therefore, a freetrader is usually the owner of an establishment, especially if it is a pub, rather than an employee. Their qualifications will depend on the actual position they hold.

Licensee

There are many different types of licensee because it is the name given to the person within an establishment in whose name the liquor licence is held. A licence is required whenever and wherever alcohol is sold, so the licensee could be a publican (see page 86) or a nightclub manager (see below) or an hotel manager (see page 26) or the principal of a higher educational establishment that has a licensed restaurant open to the general public.

A licensee does not currently need to have a particular qualification to obtain a licence. However, issuing magistrates are starting to demand that all new potential licensees must have the appropriate BII qualification, as well as proving to their satisfaction that they are honest, responsible, upright citizens who will run a well-ordered business.

Liquor licences apply to the named person at a specific place of work. If the licensee leaves, the liquor licence is invalid. For this reason there are usually two licensees for each establishment.

Management trainee
See page 28.

Nightclub manager
The role of a nightclub manager varies according to the type of establishment being managed. For example, clubs with a private membership, jazz clubs and discos are popular with different groups of people, and provide a range of entertainment. Some clubs present a cabaret act, which will mean that the manager will be responsible for booking arrangements. Others cater for functions and parties. Almost all nightclubs sell alcohol – the

manager being the licensee – and many have a food outlet, which can be anything from a snack bar to a high-class restaurant.

Staffing is another area of responsibility, from recruitment to staff organization and welfare, including bartenders and waiters, reception and the kitchen brigade. The role of a nightclub manager can be likened to many other managerial positions within the service industries.

Certain personal qualities are essential in all service areas, and the need to maintain good customer relations in this role is vital.

Unsociable hours are usual, with the majority of clubs being open until the early hours of the morning. Management must be on hand to issue floats to cashiers and bar staff and generally ensure that the club is ready for opening, which may be 9 pm. Closing time may be as late as 3 am or later in an all-night club and the manager will be needed until the customers have left, all monies having been checked and the club locked up. In addition to these hours, a manager may need to come in to do bar stocktakes and other day-time administrative duties.

BTEC or degree qualifications, in addition to experience as a bartender or bar manager, are essential.

Publican

This job can incorporate that of a freetrader (see page 84) and will always include the duties of a licensee (see page 85).

Publicans manage a pub. They may also own the pub or be a tenant of one of the brewing companies, such as Century Inns or Ushers. Even if the pub is a tenancy, it still involves most of the duties of ownership of a small business, such as hiring the staff, ordering supplies, maintenance of the building, bookkeeping, working behind the bar alongside the staff and promoting the business.

Public houses have to be open 364 days a year between the hours of approximately 11.00 am and 11.00 pm – otherwise the terms of the licence are invalidated. Therefore, people wanting to enter this profession, especially in a managerial capacity, must enjoy working long, often unsociable, hours. They must also have good social skills, be genuinely interested in people and able to work under stress.

Many bartenders (see page 83) are unqualified, but managers and assistant managers will have BTEC or HCIMA and BII qualifications, plus a great deal of experience. They may also have WSET qualifications if the pub serves a lot of wine and or food.

Sommelier
See page 37.

Telephonist
See page 99.

Waiter
See page 37.

Wine waiter
See page 38.

The employers

Unlike the administration of hotels, restaurants or travel agents, a significant number of licensed trade premises are run in a way that is unique to the UK, and to the main types of beverages sold there. This is because each country has different laws relating to the handling, sale and consumption of alcoholic drinks. Different countries may also specialize in different types of beverages. For instance, the skills learnt in a real ale pub in the UK would be transferable to a bierkeller in Germany or Denmark, but would be of little use in a café bar in France. Some companies, such as TGI Fridays, may send their top UK bar staff to America for extra training in cocktail skills, and these skills would be recognized both in America and American theme restaurants within the UK. However, they would not be immediately transferable to the cocktail bar of an up-market hotel in Lyon. This means that, having acquired bartending skills within the UK, unless you choose to work for an international chain – usually a hotel chain, such as Marriott – if you want to work overseas, you will have to learn additional skills. You would have to do the same if you had started work in a café bar in Glasgow and then chosen to work in a real ale pub in Cardiff. Thus, most people try more than one sector, but then choose to settle in one specialization.

Employers range from national (for example, Bass) and international chains, usually hotel-based chains (such as Sheraton), to independent free houses. In the chains there will be clear progression routes and training programmes. In the independent establishments, these will not exist, but you may learn very specialist skills that are of great interest to you. You might work in a wine bar and learn about sourcing, selling and serving wines, while in a CAMRA pub you may become highly skilled in the management of a traditional cellar and beer lines. Some of the large companies, such as Virgin, own hotels, nightclubs and airlines, among other things, so by working for them you may be able to experience different types of work within the same company.

Jobs in this area are often advertised in the employment section of your local paper. The more specialist jobs tend to be advertised in the relevant trade paper. For jobs in pubs, look in *The Publican*; for jobs within hotel- and restaurant-based companies, see magazines such as the *Caterer and Hotelkeeper*; jobs based solely within the wine trade can be found in magazines such as *Decanter* or *Harpers Wine and Spirit Weekly*.

Personal qualities

You will need to be physically fit. Setting up any bar means moving large quantities of stock – crates of mixers, boxes of wine, beer barrels. You also need to be sociable, outgoing, discreet, calm and tolerant, all at the same time. When people drink, they often like to chat. When they have had a little more to drink, not necessarily drunk, they may become indiscreet and tell you things that they regret later. Bar staff need to be able to understand what was 'never said' as well as remembering their regular customers' likes and dislikes. Sometimes people become drunk and then bar staff need to have the ability to remain calm, keep a volatile situation calm, or to calm an argumentative one down.

Employees in the licensed trade often work late into the night. While pubs usually close by 11 pm, nightclubs may be open to 6 am, and good hotel bars close when the last customer goes to bed. Therefore, you need to be a night person rather than someone who is good in the mornings.

Pay

Pay varies enormously. Part-time bar staff are likely to earn the national minimum wage, as is any full-time unskilled employee.

However, a bar manager on a cruise liner can earn $20,000 pa, plus tips, and has no living expenses. A freetrader can earn anything from £20,000 to £50,000, depending on the size and situation of the establishment, but many also live on the premises and have very low living costs. The manager of an off-licence would expect to make around £26,000. A tenant may make only £16,000 from their beverage sales, but can more than double that if they have significant food sales.

It should be noted that extra money is not usually paid for working unsociable hours, although many employers pay for transport home if the establishment closes very late.

Equal opportunities

The licensed trade is generally an equal opportunities employer. It is your personal skills and ability to communicate with the customers that are the most important factors in your employment, followed by your ability to work long, hard, unsociable hours and remain calm under pressure.

Many licences are held jointly by a married couple.

Those wanting to work overseas – apart from holiday resort areas – may find that some countries do have restrictions on who works where. Also, of course, some countries forbid the sale of alcohol totally, so there is no employment at all for anyone interested in the licensed trade in these countries.

Union membership

Very few people who work within the licensed trade are members of any union. This is because, at technician level, if people are unhappy, they simply change jobs, and many people who are happy with one place of employment change to another just for the variety. At management level, many people are either in training or the establishment is owner/tenant-operated. Many people belong to a variety of professional associations – which one depends on the sector they work within. For instance, many pub operators are members of the BII, those whose work is based more within the wine trade may be members of the Wine and

Spirit Association, and professional bar staff are often members of the UK Bartenders Guild.

Entry requirements and training

As previously stated, most employers will not be interested in employing anyone under the age of 18 because of the UK licensing laws. Having reached 18, many people take jobs as bartenders, often on a part-time basis, to supplement their income. Some enjoy the work and lifestyle and then move into full-time employment. This is how the vast majority of people start work within the licensed trade.

Another entry route is for mature people – generally couples – who decide that they want to change their careers. Usually, they will start by linking up with a major brewing company, with a view to becoming tenants and managing a property and, perhaps one day, owning their own establishment.

It is also becoming more common for some people who have graduated at HND or degree level, in a related discipline, to enter the industry as a management trainee. They will usually have a lot of part-time work experience and start by working for a large company because of the progression routes.

A person under 18 who knows that they want to work within the licensed trade would usually take a full-time course or Modern Apprenticeship to gain relevant qualifications and learn bar work under supervised conditions, ready for full employment by the time they reach 18.

To move into the management of any licensed premises, you will need to be eligible to hold a liquor licence. Most magistrates will not issue a licence unless the applicant has sufficient maturity – that is, you are in your late twenties or older – and sufficient knowledge of UK licensing law. Therefore, anyone seriously contemplating a career within any sector of the licensed trade within the UK would be advised to take the appropriate BII qualification.

Further information

See pages 124–37.

Chapter 5
Back-up and administrative work

The kind of work available

There are many jobs in the catering, travel and leisure industries that call for specialists, which, often, can be jobs that are found in all sectors, such as health and safety officers. The personnel/human resources department – which deals with recruitment, training and staff welfare – is similar in this respect. Some jobs, though not actually part of the industries in question, are, nevertheless, essential for an organization's efficiency. In this chapter, these types of jobs are described in detail, showing how they are associated with the industries and their importance.

The jobs

Accounts
The accounts departments in most areas already described employ bookkeepers, cashiers and credit controllers. The junior members of staff are responsible for checking the work of cashiers, preparing staff pay and maintaining a petty cash system. Staff complete purchase orders and cheques for suppliers and send invoices, reminders, statements and credit notes to customers.

Cashiers who show potential are promoted. They may already have NVQ qualifications and will often go on to take BTEC qualifications.

Senior accounts personnel may prepare medium- and long-term company budgets and provide financial assistance and information for audits. At the end of each financial year, they prepare company accounts.

Accountants and bookkeepers need professional expertise, and a thorough knowledge of the industry in which they are employed. Promotion for qualified accountants (chartered or certified, members of professional associations) may be to financial controller, a senior management position that holds responsibility for the finance of an entire company.

Army

In this book, it is not possible to go into detail about all the careers available in the Army Catering Corps and the Women's Royal Army Catering Corps, so a summary is given here. Further details of a career in any discipline of the service can be gained from *The Kogan Page Guide to Careers in the Armed Services*. The Army Catering Corps feeds the army, both in the field and in barracks, as well as on special occasions.

There are two, usually separate, career paths – one for commissioned officers and one for non-commissioned officers and other ranks. Commissioned officers usually enter the service with 'A' levels or an HND or degree in a related subject. Otherwise, the army sponsors them to obtain these qualifications. After initial basic training, an officer will be given a posting in which the catering responsibilities will be similar to those of a trainee unit manager (see page 44) and contract caterer (see page 41) combined. However, there will also be the special army-related responsibilities, such as the physical and moral care of junior ranks and the ability to operate under extreme conditions at any time. On leaving the service, most officers will find employment at the appropriate civilian rank, such as departmental manager or above.

Most other service personnel enter without any qualifications at the civilian equivalents of unskilled chef or waiter and rise through the ranks as in any other specialism. In order to progress, they often study for NVQ qualifications, which can be used once they leave the service. The career tree on page 109 shows the normal progression route for both the cook personnel and the mess (waiting) personnel. A warrant officer could easily become an hotel or area manager (see page 26), a talented a cook could become a head chef (see page 24) and mess personnel could become butlers (see page 49).

Cashier

The role of a cashier varies slightly according to the exact nature of the job. Cash handling is one of the most important jobs in any industry. Customers may pay in several ways, including cash, cheques, foreign currency, traveller's cheques, credit cards and by business accounts. The cashier has to be knowledgeable about every aspect of these means of payment. What is the currency in Italy, New Zealand or Japan? How much change has to be given? Should a cheque be accepted if it has crossings out? What is the procedure for accepting a traveller's cheque? What is a floor limit? When can a credit card be accepted? What is the procedure if a guest wants to pay in euros? Many cashiers are responsible for their employer's daily banking and therefore also have to be familiar with the necessary associated administrative tasks.

In an hotel, a cashier will be a member of the front-office team, employed as a shift worker – for example, from 7 am to 3 pm or from 3 pm to 11 pm. If the hotel caters for international and business guests, it is likely that they will need to be familiar with every method of payment.

A restaurant cashier will also have to prepare guests' bills and accept payment. A cashier for an industrial caterer will simply accept payment for meals and will often be sited at the end of a long, self-service counter. They often work part-time. A cashier in such situations also needs to be very knowledgeable. Does the organization accept vouchers? To what value? For food or drinks? Alcohol or tobacco? These are just some of the questions a cashier needs to know how to answer.

In the tourism industry, a cashier performs similar tasks. Many attractions charge entrance fees, most have catering facilities that employ cashiers, some attract foreign visitors and therefore have currency exchange facilities. A travel agency takes payment from travellers in various forms – a business traveller who may have an account with the agency, holidaymakers who pay in cash, by cheque or credit card. Many agencies have foreign exchange facilities, and as in an hotel, a cashier here needs to know about different currencies and where to find out the relevant exchange rates. A leisure centre cashier takes deposits, membership and entrance fees.

Many cashiers are employed as shift workers and, as part of their job, they have to prepare floats for the oncoming shift.

Ensuring that the next cashier has sufficient change and is not given a float entirely in large denominations can be a difficult task. In smaller establishments, the jobs of cashier, receptionist and telephonist may be combined. Wherever the job, the tasks are many and all call for personal skills in dealing with the public.

NVQ or GNVQ qualifications in an appropriate area are often essential, together with experience in cash handling. Integrity and honesty are also paramount and many employees are required to be bonded by an insurance company against any losses.

Financial controller

A financial controller is a qualified accountant, responsible for medium- and long-term budgeting, and the accounts department. This position is the most senior within a financial department. Many accountants will progress to general management roles in large corporations.

They will be qualified in accountancy work, or a related discipline, and will have entered the industry with an HND or degree and have many years' experience.

Health and safety officer

All organizations that employ more than five people have to have an official health and safety policy to protect their employees and customers. In large organizations, a specialist post is created – that of health and safety officer. This is a supervisory position or above, designed to set up and run the company health and safety policy and conduct training to ensure that all staff are aware of the correct – safe – work practices.

A health and safety officer is likely to be attached to a human resources department, but their background may be in any sector of the industry. They will have several years' experience of working within the industry and are also likely to have taken the Royal Society of Health (RSH) Diploma.

Home economist

Many home economists have other job titles, such as project researcher or customer adviser, but all the jobs have a similar content – to test, demonstrate and research new equipment and food products for the domestic market. They might work for one of the gas companies and test out new equipment to see how it reacts under various circumstances or demonstrate the items to potential customers on site in a restaurant or demonstration area.

Most home economists need to have good social skills because of the high level of customer contact. They also usually have BTEC or degree qualifications, often in Consumer Sciences.

Human resources

This department/area is concerned with the people – the personnel – who work for an organization. In general, it is concerned with the recruitment, welfare, training and retention of staff in a company. By employing a person (or people) to organize and oversee these functions, other departments can concentrate on providing a service and running the organization without worrying about staff problems. The number of people employed in a personnel department will depend largely on the size and type of organization and the number of employees.

There are three main functions of a human resources department, which are administration, recruitment and training. Each of these specialist areas is handled by one or more people in a large organization (250 or more employees), and the department headed by a human resources manager. However, in a smaller establishment, two or more of the roles may be combined into one position.

The responsibilities of a human resource manager are mainly administrative, and include compiling and maintaining employees' files, monitoring and controlling sickness, absence and holidays, dealing with pay queries, writing job descriptions, creating and administering induction and training programmes, preparing contracts of employment and administering employee benefit schemes. Depending on the size and structure of a human resource department, a human resource manager may be involved in staff disciplinary and grievance procedures, although this responsibility may be taken by unit management in some organizations. In small companies, there may be one human resource employee, responsible for all the functions involved under the 'personnel' umbrella. In this situation, a human resource manager may also actually run training sessions themselves, their job becoming more 'hands on'.

In any job within a human resource department, personality and personal abilities are important. Good communication skills and a positive attitude are also essential, as a fair but firm approach to the job in hand is required. The ability to keep confidences is also necessary.

A Hospitality Management HND or degree usually provides basic administrative skills and knowledge about the specific industry required. In order to progress to the level of a human resource manager, experience of administrative duties is required, and often a professional personnel management qualification. The Institute of Personnel Management (IPM) course takes two years part-time (evenings or days) if you have a degree qualification, or three years if you do not. The course can also be taken as a one-year full-time postgraduate course. However, a qualification in office administration can also helpful in obtaining a first administrative job within a human resources department.

Another area of responsibility may be that of recruitment. See below for further information.

Lecturer

In further and higher education, the vast majority of lecturers have worked for many years within the industry before they start to teach their specialisms. This is especially true in the vocational areas of hospitality and the licensed trade as these are service industries needing a practical approach. Once experienced, they enter the teaching profession and usually study for a teaching qualification on a full- or part-time basis. This, in addition to their specialist qualification, is necessary in order to progress.

Personnel officer

See Human resources, page 95, and Recruitment officer, page 97.

Public relations officer

A public relations officer will often be part of the marketing team, and their role is to present their organization in a favourable light to enhance its reputation. They will be called on to write press releases or be responsible for advertising a forthcoming event or attraction. Much of the work will involve meeting journalists and photographers, answering enquiries or researching information. It is a skilful job that involves dealing with people, working under pressure and sometimes unsociable hours.

NVQ and GNVQ courses frequently include the necessary key communication skills. BTEC courses, in relevant disciplines, also include valuable skills for those wishing to pursue a career in this field. The professional organization is the Communication Advertising and Marketing Education Foundation, which is an examining body.

Purchasing officer
Larger organizations may employ a purchasing officer. As the job title suggests, a purchasing officer is responsible for all purchases. The job will involve buying everything from capital equipment and furniture to uniforms and stationery, and making purchases for resale. Purchasing officers have to liaise with suppliers, research new products, communicate with other departments; they may also act as storekeepers in small establishments when deliveries and requisitions are made and ensure that the quality and quantities are correct.

Depending on the organization structure, a purchasing officer may be responsible for signing new contracts with suppliers and continually try to find new suppliers to provide a more competitive service.

An ideal candidate will have experience of the hospitality industry, together with a relevant BTEC qualification.

Recruitment officer
In larger companies, the responsibility for recruiting staff will be left to one specialist employee. A recruitment officer will be required to organize and design recruitment advertising, screen application forms, carry out a selection interview for all applicants, follow up references for prospective employees, control a recruitment budget, source new methods of recruitment and monitor and control departmental transfers and promotions. They must also ensure that all applicants are written to with the results of their interviews and give careers advice/information at college/school open days.

During quiet spells, a recruitment officer is also directly involved in other functions within a human resource department. In order to be fully effective, a recruitment officer needs to have a thorough understanding of all the jobs in the company. Therefore, previous practical experience is a great benefit, and will make explaining a job to a prospective employee easier.

BTEC or degree qualifications provide a sound grounding for a recruitment officer, along with practical personnel experience of the organization and its procedures. In most companies, before being given the responsibility of interviewing staff, an officer is sent on a training course to learn this specialist skill. An officer intending to progress within this area would normally take the IPM examinations on a full- or part-time basis.

Royal Air Force
It is not appropriate to describe here all the catering ranks. For further information, contact your nearest RAF Careers Information Office. In summary, there are four main areas to consider and each one can be related to a civilian counterpart, always bearing in mind the extra duties of service personnel with respect to nutrition, physical and moral health, security and so on. The career trees on pages 119 and 120 demonstrate these connections clearly.

Ordinary airmen and airwomen and non-commissioned officers usually follow one of three paths: they specialize as chefs, entering the service as unskilled trainees, gaining NVQ qualifications to enable them to rise, possibly as far as the rank of warrant officer with skills equivalent to those of an area manager or executive chef (see pages 92 and 24); they enter as clerks, or storemen (see catering clerk, page 41); they specialize in the waiting, or mess, section and here, like chef aircraft personnel, they take NVQ qualifications to enable them to rise through the ranks, possibly as far as warrant officer, which equates to a general managerial position in civilian life, although many stewards enter private service when they leave the Air Force.

Commissioned officers have a degree or HND in a related subject on entry and progress through various managerial positions that enable them to obtain senior management positions on leaving the service.

Sales and marketing manager
As part of a sales and marketing department, a sales and marketing manager may be employed by an hotel, a restaurant chain, tourist board or local authority. A marketing team within an organization creates a demand for something that can then be sold by the sales staff. The team brings suppliers together in order to produce a unique package that fills a gap in the market. The department has to find ways of making the public interested in the area, product or service and make it appear different from

the competition's products or services. This can mean promoting special kinds of holidays, such as murder/mystery weekends, adventure holidays for the over fifties or organizing promotions for the businessperson – ensuring that it is their company's beer that the VIP is filmed drinking.

Responsibilities include planning and preparing promotions and presentations, assessing competition within the same market or location, gathering information on facilities and attractions within the area, organizing displays at exhibitions and arranging conferences. The members of a sales and marketing team often meet members of the public, so they need to have outgoing personalities, together with the ability to work under pressure.

A good BTEC or degree qualification is essential, and often those wishing to pursue a career in this area work to gain higher-level specialist qualifications from the Institute of Marketing.

Secretarial and clerical work

Secretarial and clerical staff are employed by all medium-sized to large establishments or companies. Many senior members of staff (for example, a financial controller or managing director) have their own secretary. Other secretaries work for a small group of people. They need up-to-date IT and word processing skills, good educational qualifications, common sense, initiative and a good telephone manner. Junior members of staff may be responsible for sorting mail, photocopying, filing and acting as messengers.

Switchboard

See Telephonist, below.

Telephonist

A telephonist or switchboard operator is often considered to be the most important person in a service industry. Like a receptionist, who is the first person clients see, a telephonist may be the first person outsiders speak to. Telephonist jobs have sometimes been given to junior members of staff in order to keep them away from public areas, in the mistaken belief that no harm can be done, but, in fact, potential sales may be lost as a result of an error by a telephonist who fails to answer a caller correctly, does not transfer a caller immediately, leaves a caller on hold or gives them wrong information.

In many establishments, the role of telephonist is combined with that of receptionist. A good telephone manner is essential. Experience of different switchboard systems is sometimes gained on an in-house training programme, although a Reception or Front-of-house Studies NVQ qualification is advantageous.

Training officer

In any organization, staff training is important in order to ensure that everyone is aware of their responsibilities and how to give good service to a customer. Most large companies within the hospitality and licensed trade industry employ full-time training officers who are responsible for ensuring that staff receive training in respect of their particular needs.

The duties of a training officer include organizing and carrying out training courses, holding induction training for new staff, planning future training events and requirements, controlling training budgets and expenditure, monitoring job training carried out in each department of the company, placing industrial release students from colleges and giving careers advice and guidance to employees and to schools/ colleges. In some smaller organizations, a training officer may combine their role with that of another personnel function.

Formal qualifications from one of the hospitality disciplines at BTEC level or above, plus experience in either training administration or in a human resource department, are essential. It is important that training staff are themselves aware of the workings of the other areas of the company and therefore practical experience in these areas is essential. The Hospitality Training Foundation offers a range of training courses designed to teach training skills. Most training officers have received this form of training, and then from this level there are further courses of study available in order to gain other professional qualifications.

Entry requirements and training

Qualifications, training and experience are clearly a necessity when applying for a professional position. Most organizations will train their employees, however, when the work involves a specialist skill or in order for them to keep up to date with new developments, such as in the use of information technology or after promotion to a higher-level job with more responsibility. In other organizations, employees will have to gain more qualifications in their own time. In either case, this is usually via a part-time course of study or distance learning.

Further information

See pages 124–37.

Chapter 6
Courses available

Listed below is a range of the courses/areas of study at present available within the UK that will lead to a recognized qualification within the hospitality and licensed trade industries. At HND, degree and postgraduate level, many courses are now modular, tailored to individual requirements. As these courses are so individual, you will need to check with UCAS or the university concerned as to the exact area of study and title of the course/s you are interested in.

British Airways

- The Academy of Travel Management, Ticketing Course

Business and Technology Education Council (BTEC) and Scottish Vocational Education Council (SCOTVEC)

BTEC
GNVQ Foundation or First Certificates:

- Hospitality and Catering
- Leisure and Tourism

GNVQ Intermediate or First Diplomas:

- Hospitality and Catering
- Leisure and Tourism

National Certificates:

- Hotel, Catering and Institutional Operations
- Hotel, Catering and Institutional Operations (Accommodation Operations)
- Hotel, Catering and Institutional Operations (Catering Operations)
- Hotel, Catering and Institutional Operations (Food and Drink Service)
- Hotel, Catering and Institutional Operations (Front-office Operations)
- Hotel, Catering and Institutional Operations (Housekeeping)
- Hotel, Catering and Institutional Operations (Housekeeping and Catering)
- Leisure Studies
- Travel and Tourism

GNVQ Advanced and National Diplomas:

- Business and Finance, Hotel, Catering and Travel Administration Options
- Hospitality and Catering
- Hotel, Catering and Institutional Operations (European Division)
- Hotel, Catering and Institutional Operations (Vegetarian Catering)
- Leisure and Tourism

Higher National Certificates:

- Hospitality Management
- Licensed Trade
- Recreation and Leisure
- Tourism

Higher National Diplomas:

- Catering Management
- Food Technology Studies
- Hospitality Management

- Hotel, Catering and Institutional Management
- Leisure Management/Studies
- Licensed Trade Management
- Recreation Management/Studies
- Tourism/Tourism Studies/Management
- Travel/Travel Management

SCOTVEC
National Certificate Modules:

- Business and Administration Group (Hotel Management)
- Business and Administration Group (Supervision of Catering)
- Food Services Group (Food/Beverages Services)
- Hotel Catering and Institutional Operations
- Industrial Processing Group (General Catering)
- Supervision of Catering and Accommodation Services
- Travel and Tourism

Higher National Certificate:

- Hospitality Management
- Leisure Studies
- Recreation Studies
- Travel and Tourism

Higher National Diploma:

- Business Studies (Travel and Tourism)
- Catering Management
- Hospitality Management
- Hotel Services Management
- Hotel, Catering and Institutional Management

National Vocational Qualifications/Scottish Vocational Qualifications NVQ/SVQ

- Accommodation Supervision   Level 3
- Accommodation Management   Level 4
- Drinks Service – Advanced Craft   Level 3
- Food and Drink Service – Bar Service   Levels 1 and 2

- Food and Drink Service – Counter/Takeaway — Level 1
- Food and Drink Service – Functions — Level 2
- Food and Drink Service – Table Service — Level 1 And 2
- Food and Drink Service – Vending — Level 1
- Food Preparation and Cooking — Levels 1 and 2
- Food Service – Advanced Craft — Level 3
- Front-office Management — Level 4
- Front-office Supervision — Level 3
- Guest Service — Levels 1 and 2
- Housekeeping — Levels 1 and 2
- Kitchen and Larder Specialist — Level 4
- Kitchen and Larder Work — Level 3
- Kitchen Portering — Level 1
- Kitchen Supervision — Level 3
- Multiskilled Hospitality Management — Level 4
- Multiskilled Hospitality Supervision — Level 3
- On-licensed Premises Management — Level 4
- On-licensed Premises Supervision — Level 3
- Patisserie and Confectionery Specialist — Level 4
- Patisserie and Confectionery — Level 3
- Portering — Level 1
- Preparing and Serving Food – Quick Service — Level 2
- Preparing and Serving Food — Level 1
- Reception — Levels 1 and 2
- Restaurant Management — Level 4
- Restaurant Supervision — Level 3
- Vegetarian — Level 3

Degrees

- Arts Administration
- Business Studies
- Catering Management
- Catering and Applied Nutrition
- Consumer Science
- Dietetics
- Food and Accommodation Management
- Food Technology
- Gallery Studies
- Hospitality Management

- Hotel Administration
- Hotel and Catering Administration
- Hotel and Catering Business
- Hotel and Catering Management
- Hotel and Tourism Management
- Hotel Catering and Institutional Administration
- Hotel Catering and Institutional Management
- Human Nutrition and Dietetics
- Institutional Management
- International Hotel Management
- Leisure and Tourism Management
- Leisure Management
- Leisure Services and Tourism
- Leisure Studies
- Museums and Gallery Administration
- Nutrition and Dietetics
- Recreation Management
- Sport and Leisure Studies
- Sport and Recreation Studies
- Tourism
- Tourism Marketing
- Tourism Planning and Development
- Tourism Studies
- Travel and Tourism

Students should note that a BSc degree will be much more science based than a BA, and that an honours (hons) degree is a level higher than an ordinary degree. As previously stated, this list is a range of subject areas rather than a list of degree-level courses. Students looking to do a postgraduate course will need to contact the relevant university directly.

Hotel and Catering International Management Association

- The Professional Certificate
- The Professional Diploma

Wine and Spirit Education Trust

- Certificate in Wines and Associated Beverages
- Higher Certificate in Wines, Spirits and Liqueurs
- Diploma in Wines, Spirits and Liqueurs

British Institute of Innkeeping

- National Licensee's Certificate (Off-licence)
- National Licensee's Certificate (On-licence)
- National Licensee's Certificate (Part IV Licences)

Royal Institute of Public Health and Hygiene

- Primary Certificate
- Certificate in Food Hygiene
- Diploma in Food Hygiene – Advanced Level
- Certificate in Nutrition and Health

Chapter 7
Career trees

The 'trees' that have been reproduced on the following pages are diagrammatical and not exact career progression tables. The reason for this is that, although many large establishments and companies have this kind of formalized career structure, there are many small and privately owned businesses where several jobs are combined. If you choose to work in a small establishment, you will be expected to be able to do several jobs. If it is your own business, you should be able to do them all!

Notice also how easy it is at different stages to change from one career path to another. Don't be afraid that you may choose the wrong job and be stuck with that career for ever. You won't be; changing is that easy. In the hospitality and licensed trade industry, once you have the basic qualifications, experience is just as important for promotion as your higher-level qualifications. Higher-level qualifications simply mean that you start higher up the tree or climb it a little quicker. In the end, whether you succeed or not depends on you and your personality.

The unbroken lines on the career trees indicate the normal path and the broken lines indicate where changes quite commonly occur. Cross-references give tree numbers.

1. Academic Staff

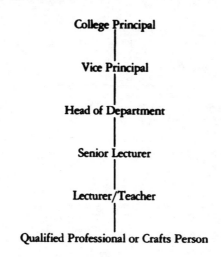

College Principal

Vice Principal

Head of Department

Senior Lecturer

Lecturer/Teacher

Qualified Professional or Crafts Person

2. Army Catering Corps

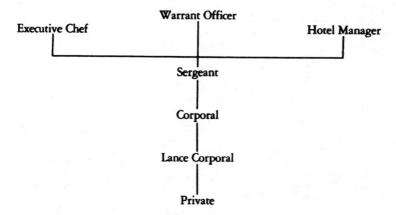

Executive Chef

Warrant Officer

Hotel Manager

Sergeant

Corporal

Lance Corporal

Private

The chain is followed whether you choose to follow the cookery or waiting side. If you become a chef you will be able to specialise, ie larder, pastry, ice carving, etc. If you become a steward/ess you will be able to gain a knowledge of wines and spirits as well as waiting.

Commissioned Officer. Generally you would need an HND or degree to start at this level. See page 92.

3. Banqueting/Conference Management

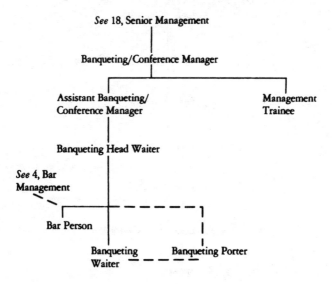

4. Bar Management

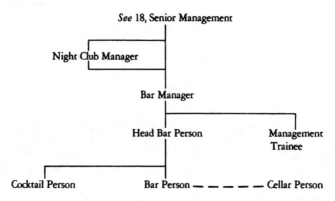

5. Financial Management

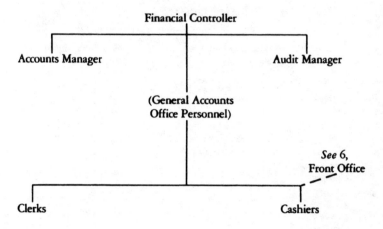

Financial Controller

Accounts Manager

Audit Manager

(General Accounts
Office Personnel)

See 6,
Front Office

Clerks

Cashiers

6. Front Office Management

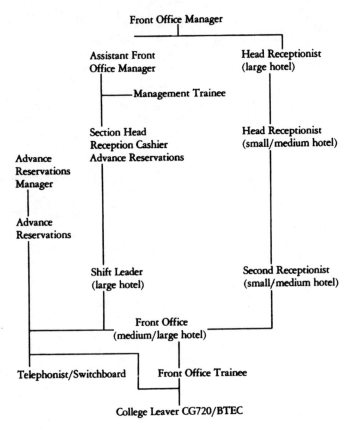

7. Home Economist

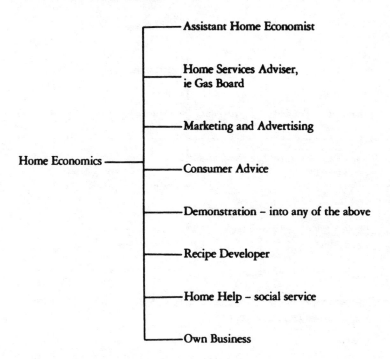

Many people who study home economics do not enter into the mainstream of the industry, but branch off into one of the above.

8. Housekeeping/Accommodation Services

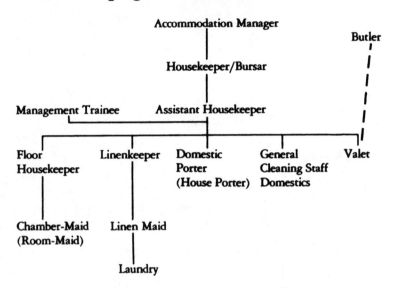

A housekeeper is the term used in hotels. A bursar is the term used in colleges/halls of residence, etc.

9. Kitchen Brigade

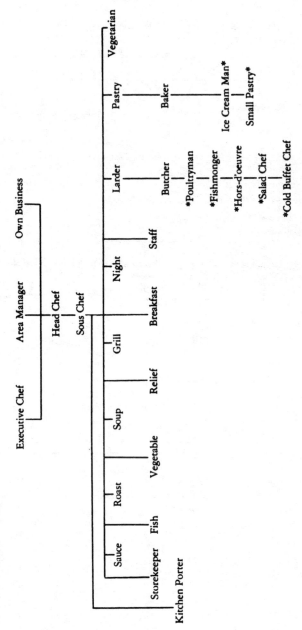

*These are specialist chefs often not found in modern-day kitchens, although section leaders will have all these skills.

10. Master of Ceremonies

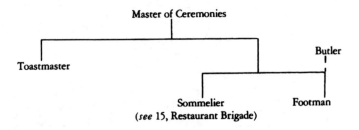

11. Personnel

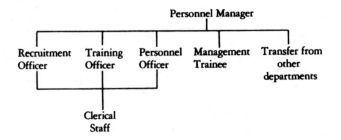

12. Public Relations

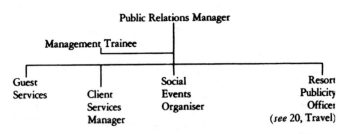

13. Publican/Innkeeper/Licensee

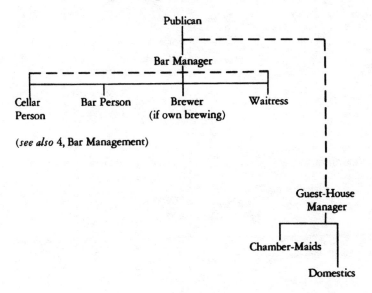

(*see also* 4, Bar Management)

14. Purchasing Management

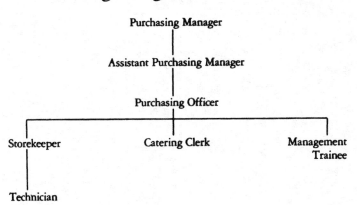

15. Restaurant Brigade

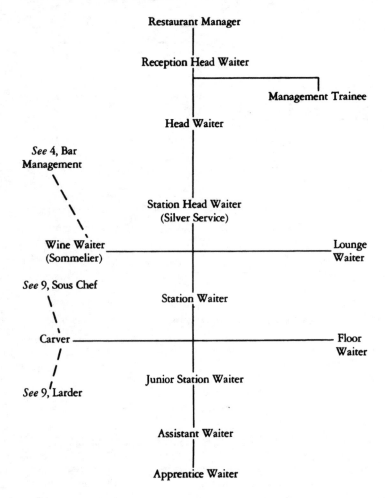

Restaurant Manager

Reception Head Waiter

Management Trainee

Head Waiter

See 4, Bar Management

Station Head Waiter (Silver Service)

Wine Waiter (Sommelier)

Lounge Waiter

See 9, Sous Chef

Station Waiter

Carver

Floor Waiter

See 9, Larder

Junior Station Waiter

Assistant Waiter

Apprentice Waiter

16. Royal Air Force catering

(a) Cook/Chef

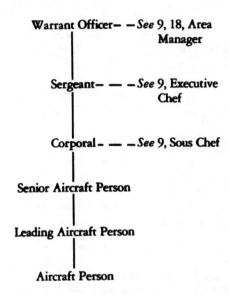

Warrant Officer— —*See* 9, 18, Area Manager

Sergeant— — —*See* 9, Executive Chef

Corporal— — —*See* 9, Sous Chef

Senior Aircraft Person

Leading Aircraft Person

Aircraft Person

(b) Catering Clerk

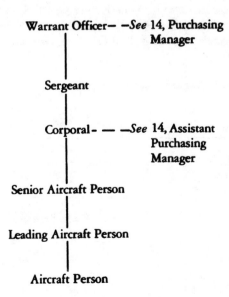

Warrant Officer— —*See* 14, Purchasing Manager

Sergeant

Corporal— — —*See* 14, Assistant Purchasing Manager

Senior Aircraft Person

Leading Aircraft Person

Aircraft Person

(c) Steward/Mess Manager

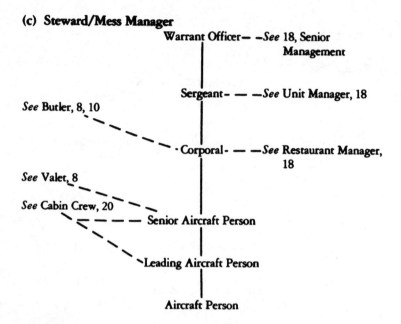

(d) Commissioned Officer

A commissioned officer would start at the level of Deputy Catering Officer (see Management Trainee, 3, 4, 6, 8, 15.) You need one of the following: HCIMA Part B, degree, HND, OND or BTEC, plus O levels or GCSEs at grade A, B or C in five other subjects.

17. Sales and Marketing

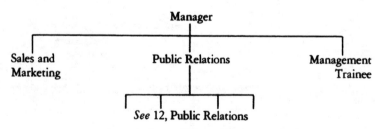

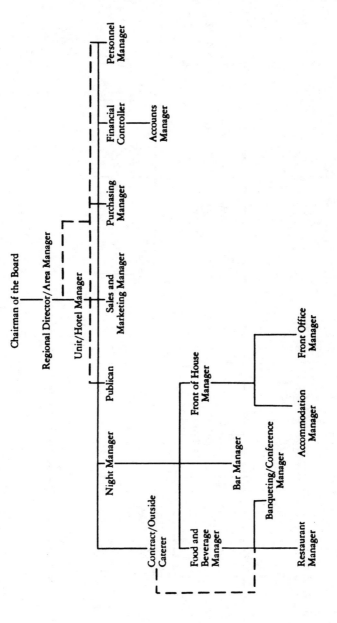

18. Senior Management

Career trees

19. Tourism

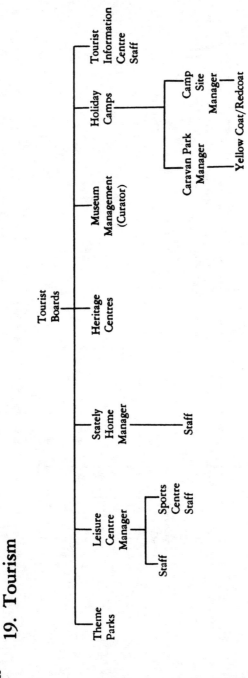

Any of the above could be called Amenity Manager or Entertainment Centre Manager.

20. Travel

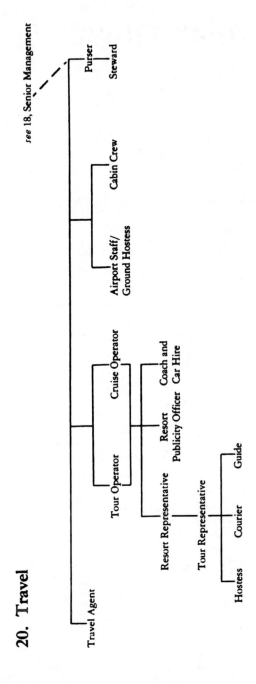

see 18, Senior Management

Travel Agent

Tour Operator — Cruise Operator

Resort Representative

Resort Publicity Officer — Coach and Car Hire

Tour Representative

Hostess — Courier — Guide

Airport Staff/ Ground Hostess — Cabin Crew

Purser — Steward

Further information

Useful addresses

Always send a self-addressed, stamped envelope when you write off for information.

ABTA National Training Board
Waterloo House
11–17 Chertsey Road
Woking
Surrey GU21 5AL
Tel: 01483 727321

Army School of Catering Headquarters
St Omar Barracks
Aldershot
Hampshire GU11 2BN
Tel: 01252 348184

Association for Conferences and Events (ACE International)
Riverside House
High Street
Huntingdon
Cambridgeshire PE18 6SG
Tel: 01480 457595

Association of British Travel Agents
55–57 Newman Street
London W1P 4AH
Tel: 0171 637 2444

Association of Domestic Management
3 Hagg Bank Cottages
Wylam
Northumberland NE41 8JT
Tel: 01661 853097

Association of Licensed Free Traders
Dane House
55 London Road
St Albans
Hertfordshire AL1 1LJ
Tel: 01727 841644

Association of Teachers in Travel and Tourism (ATTT)
c/o Tourism Society
26 Chapter Street
London SW1P 4ND
Tel: 0171 834 0461

Brewers and Licensed Retailers Association
42 Portman Square
London W1H 0BB
Tel: 0171 486 4831

British Association of Hotel Accountants
The Inbye
Watsons Lane
Norwood
near Harrogate
North Yorkshire HG3 1TE
Tel: 01943 880480

British Association of Conference Destinations
1st Floor
Elizabeth House
22 Suffolk Street
Queensway
Birmingham B1 1LS
Tel: 0121 616 1400

Further information

British Dietetic Association
7th Floor
Elizabeth House
22 Suffolk Street
Queensway
Birmingham Bl 1LS
Tel: 0121 643 5483

British Franchise Association (BFA)
Thames View
Newton Road
Henley on Thames
Oxfordshire RG9 1HG
Tel: 01491 578049

British Hospitality Association
Queens House
55–60 Lincoln's Inn Fields
London WC2A 3BH
Tel: 0171 404 7744

British Incoming Tour Operators Association
Vigilant House
120 Wilton Road
London SW1V 1JZ
Tel: 0171 931 0601

British Institute of Cleaning Science
Whitworth Chambers
George Row
Northampton NN1 1DF
Tel: 01604 230075

British Institute of Innkeeping
Park House
24 Park Street
Camberley
Surrey GU15 3PL
Tel: 01276 684449

British Nutrition Foundation
High Holborn House
52–54 High Holborn
London WC1V 6RQ
Tel: 0171 404 6504

British Resorts Association
8 Post Office Avenue
Southport
Merseyside PR9 0US
Tel: 0151 934 2286

British Safety Council
70 Chancellors Road
London W6 9RS
Tel: 0181 741 1231

British Standards Institution (BSI)
389 Chiswick High Road
London W4 4AL
Tel: 0181 996 9000

British Tourist Authority
Thames Tower
Black's Road
London W6 9EL
Tel: 0181 846 9000

Business and Technology Education Council (BTEC)
Central House
Upper Woburn Place
London WC1H 0HH
Tel: 0171 413 8400

Campaign for Real Ale Limited (CAMRA)
230 Hatfield Road
St Albans
Hertfordshire AL1 4LW
Tel: 01727 867201

Further information

Camping and Outdoor Leisure Association
Moritt House
58 Station Approach
South Ruislip
Middlesex HA4 6SA
Tel: 0181 842 1111

Catering Managers Association of Great Britain and the Channel
Islands
Mount Pleasant
Egton
Whitby
North Yorkshire YO12 1UE
Tel: 01947 895514

Chartered Institute of Environmental Health
Chadwick Court
15 Hatfields
London SE1 8DJ
Tel: 0171 928 6006

Chartered Institute of Management Accountants
63 Portland Place
London W1N 4AB
Tel: 0171 637 2311

Chartered Institute of Marketing
Moor Hall
Cookham
Maidenhead
Berkshire SL6 9QH
Tel: 01628 4275000

Chartered Institute of Purchasing and Supply
Easton House
Easton-on-the-Hill
Stamford
Lincolnshire PE9 3NZ
Tel: 01780 56777

City and Guilds
1 Giltspur Street
London EC1A 9DD
Tel: 0171 294 2468

Confederation of Tourism Hotel and Catering Management
204 Barnet Wood Lane
Ashtead
Surrey KT21 2DB
Tel: 01372 278572

Countryside Commission
John Dower House
Crescent Place
Cheltenham
Gloucestershire GL50 3RA
Tel: 01242 521381

Department of National Heritage
2–4 Cockspur Street
London SW1Y 5DH
Tel: 0171 211 6324

EDEXCEL Foundation
Stewart House
32 Russell Square
London WC1B 5DN
Tel: 0171 393 4444

European Catering Association (GB)
Bourne House
Horsell Park
Woking
Surrey GU21 4LY
Tel: 01483 765111

European Tour Operators Association
Fulton House
Fulton Road
Empire Way
Wembley
Middlesex HA9 0TF
Tel: 0181 902 8998

Event Services Association
8 Home Farm
Ardington
Oxfordshire OX12 8BG
Tel: 01235 821820

Federation of Bakers
20 Bedford Square
London WC2B 5JJ
Tel: 0171 580 4252

Federation of Small Business (FSB)
2 Catherine Place
Westminster
London SW1E 6HF
Tel: 0171 233 7900

Health and Safety Executive (HSE)
Rose Court
2 Southwark Bridge
London SE1 9HS
Tel: 0171 717 6000

Health Education Authority
Trevelyan House
30 Great Peter Street
London SW1P 2HW
Tel: 0171 222 5300

HM Customs and Excise
New Kings Beam House
22 Upper Ground
London SE1 9PJ
Tel: 0171 620 1313

Hospital Caterers Association
c/o Facilities Directorate
Keycol Hospital
Newington
Sittingbourne
Kent ME9 8NG
Tel: 01295 842222

Hospitality Information Technology Association (Europe) (HITA)
School of Tourism and Hospitality Management
Leeds Metropolitan University
Calverley Street
Leeds LS1 3HE
Tel: 0113 283 3436

Hospitality Training Foundation
International House
High Street
Ealing
London W5 5DB
Tel: 0181 579 2400

Hotel Catering and International Management Association
(HCIMA)
191 Trinity Road
London SWI7 7HN
Tel: 0181 672 4251

Institute of Brewing
33 Clarges Street
London W1Y 8EE
Tel: 0171 499 8144

Institute of Careers Guidance
27a Lower High Street
Stourbridge
West Midlands DY8 1TA
Tel: 01384 376464

Institute of Chartered Accountants in England and Wales
(ICAEW)
Chartered Accountants' Hall
PO Box 433
Moorgate Place
London EC2P 2BJ
Tel: 0171 920 8100

Institute of Chartered Accountants in Ireland
87–89 Pembroke Road
Ballsbridge
Dublin 4
Republic of Ireland
Tel: 353 (1) 668 0400

Institute of Chartered Accountants of Scotland
27 Queen Street
Edinburgh EH2 lLA
Tel: 0131 225 5673

Institute of Food Science and Technology
5 Cambridge Court
210 Shepherd's Bush Road
London W6 7NL
Tel: 0171 603 6316

Institute of Health Services Management
39 Charlton Street
London NW1 1JD
Tel: 0171 388 2626

Institute of Home Economics
21 Portland Place
London W1N 3AF
Tel: 0171 436 5677

Institute of Hotel Security Management
PO Box 3427
London NW1 67F

Institute of Leisure and Amenity Management
ILAM House
Lower Basildon
Reading
Berkshire RG8 9NE
Tel: 01491 874222

Institute of Management
Management House
Cottingham Road
Corby
Northamptonshire NN17 1TT
Tel: 01536 204222

The Institute of Masters of Wine
Five Kings House
1 Queen Place
London EC4R 1QS
Tel: 0171 236 4427

Institute of Occupational Safety and Health (IOSH)
The Grange
Highfield Drive
Wigston
Leicestershire LE18 1NN
Tel: 0116 257 1399

Institute of Personnel and Development
IPD House
35 Camp Road
Wimbledon
London SW19 4UX
Tel: 0181 971 9000

Institute of Purchasing Management
Purchasing House
1 Fox Lane
Little Bookham
Surrey KT23 3AT
Tel: 01372 454131

Institute of Sales and Marketing Management
31 Upper George Street
Luton
Bedfordshire LU1 2RD
Tel: 01582 411130

Institute of Travel and Tourism Limited
113 Victoria Street
St Albans
Hertfordshire AL1 3TJ
Tel: 01727 854395

International Brewers Guild
8 Ely Place
Holborn
London EC1N 6SD
Tel: 0171 405 4565

The International Wine and Food Society
9 Fitzmaurice Place
Berkeley Square
London W1X 6JD
Tel: 0171 495 4191

Ivor Spencer International School for Butler Administrators/
Personal Assistants
12 Little Bornes
Alleyn Park
Dulwich
London SE21 8SE
Tel: 0181 670 5585

Mobile and Outside Caterers Association (Great Britain) Limited
Centre Court
1301 Stratford Road
Hall Green
Birmingham B28 9HH
Tel: 0121 693 7000

National Association of Licensed House Managers
Charlton House
7 Wilson Patten Street
Warrington
Cheshire WA1 1PG
Tel: 01925 244888

National Council for Vocational Qualifications (NCVQ)
222 Euston Road
London NW1 2BZ
Tel: 0171 387 9898

National Outdoor Events Association
7 Hamilton Way
Wallington
Surrey SM6 9NJ
Tel: 0181 669 8121

Northern Council for Further Education (NCFE)
5 Grosvenor Villas
Grosvenor Road
Newcastle Upon Tyne NE2 2RU
Tel: 0191 281 3242

Restaurateurs' Association of Great Britain
28 Kingsway
London WC2B 6JR
Tel: 0171 831 8727

Royal Society of Health (RSH)
RSH House
38a St George's Drive
London SW1V 4BH
Tel: 0171 630 0121

Scottish Vocational Education Council (SCOTVEC)
Hanover House
24 Douglas Street
Glasgow G2 7NQ
Tel: 0141 248 7900

Sports Council
16 Upper Woburn Place
London WC1H 0QP
Tel: 0171 388 1277

Springboard
1–3 Denmark Street
London WC2H 8LP
Tel: 0171 497 8654

Tourism Society
26 Chapter Street
London SW1P 4ND
Tel: 0171 834 0461

UK Bartenders Guild
74 Enfield Road
Blackpool
Lancashire FY1 2RB
Tel: 01253 295534

United Kingdom Vineyards Association
Church Road
Bruisyard
Saxmundham
Suffolk IP17 2EF
Tel: 01728 638080

Universities and Colleges Admissions Service (UCAS)
PO Box 67
Cheltenham
Gloucestershire GL50 3SF
Tel: 01242 222444

Wine and Spirit Association of Great Britain and Northern
Ireland
Five Kings House
1 Queen Street Place
London EC4R 1QS
Tel: 0171 248 5377

Wine and Spirit Education Trust
Five Kings House
1 Queen Street Place
London EC4R 1QS
Tel: 0171 236 3551

World Travel and Tourism Council (WTTC)
20 Grosvenor Place
London SW1X 7TT
Tel: 0171 838 9400

Further reading

Careers in Catering and Hotel Management, Russell Joseph, 5th edition (Kogan Page)
Careers in Sport, Louise Fyffe, 7th edition (Kogan Page)
Careers in the Travel Industry, Verité Reily Collins, 6th edition (Kogan Page)
Great Careers for People Interested in Travel and Tourism, Donna Sharon and Jo Anne Summers (Kogan Page)

Only a few of the following periodicals carry job advertisements, but they are all about leisure:

Baths Service & Recreational Management
Body Talk
British Journal of Physical Education
Leisure Management
The Leisure Manager
Leisure News
Sport and Leisure
Sports Industry
Swimming Pool
Tourism

Index

Abbreviations used can be found on page ix